AF483731

CHURCH AND STATE

APPOLLES SWEATTE

CHURCH AND STATE
Copyright © 2024 Appolles Sweatte.

No part of this publication may be reproduced, distributed, or transmitted in any form or by any means, including photocopying, recording, or other electronic or mechanical methods, without the prior written permission of the publisher, except in the case of brief quotations embodied in reviews and certain other non-commercial uses permitted by copyright law.

Authorunit
17130 Van Buren Blvd., Ste. 238,
Riverside, CA 92504
877-826-5888
www.authorunit.com

Because of the dynamic nature of the Internet, any web addresses or links contained in this book may have changed since publication and may no longer be valid. The views expressed in the work are solely those of the author and do not necessarily reflect the views of the publisher, and the publisher hereby disclaims any responsibility for them.

Any people depicted in stock imagery provided by Getty images are models, and such images are being used for illustrative purposes only.

ISBN 979-8-89030-406-3 (Paperback)
ISBN 979-8-89030-456-8 (Ebook)

Printed in the United States of America

Contents

TOPICAL WRITINGS

DESIGNED TO BE PROVACATIVE & INSTRUCTIVE

- ALL WILL KNOW THAT WE ARE HIS IF WE LOVE
- CURRENT EVENTS
- VOTER DEMANDS
- LOOKING BACK; GOING FORWARD
- CHOOSING THE RIGHT PLATFORM

CONCEPT of CHURCH and STATE IN PERSPECTIVE

(1) The "church" is defined as "the body of Christ" (called out and called together) One may be in the state, but not in the church. A citizen of the state or country whom is in the church is not in the church by virtue of the constitution. The constitution derived its excellence from those called out by virtue of a higher calling. Therefore the constitution is replete with biblical knowledge.

"Öur constitution was made only for a moral and religious people it is wholly inadequate to the government of any other" (Church & State P. 11). "The founders also realized that a moral society comes from children who learn the Bible".

The concept of "separation of church and state" is not "interpretation", it's "accommodation" it is finding a way to satisfy a complaint. The constitution cannot be properly interpreted without a biblical background.

(2) You can be in the State and not in the Church, but cannot be in the Church but not in Christ so, if you are in Christ, you don't step out of Christ or (the church) because you are on government property. If this then is considered religion, the State is privileged to violate the constitution by imposing a restriction on certain religious practices held by the silent majority.

Let's not blame the State because the church is silent

THE TRUE CONSTITUTIONAL POSITION ON THE "EXERCISE CLAUSE"

The State has formed all kinds of institutions and departments: Law enforcement, Health, Commerce, all kinds of civil services are regulated and given guidelines to follow. But the church is left to the Minister. Congress would make no laws regulating or choosing doctrine or preferring one over the other. The church should have been involved in the Court's decision briefs or something should have been filed to consider all the people not just Madelyn O'Hara.

The church should demand that the ten commandments are given back to the school especially.

When it comes to prayer in school, although we have been able to invoke certain practices such as "pledge of allegiance", our national anthem, rather successfully, with minimum objection, prayer may involve myriad details including posture, position, language and things with which agreement is made impossible. The simplest prayer "God Bless America" is generally accepted everywhere and honors "God" our "Creator" who endow us with inalienable rights, includes government, families, schools, religion, and society as a whole, everyone can ask God's blessing on their lives. The appeal to conscience and brotherhood and sisterhood, will accomplish far more than all the laws and court decisions written. Self respect and respect for our fellowman begins with FAITH. GIVE AMERICA FAITH AGAIN.

Nadie verá esto en el feed a menos que lo compartas

INTRODUCTION

The initial context of this history and foundation is the story of a people in search of peace and freedom consistent with their faith in the One True God. The spirit that drove them was efficacious and graceful in bringing them through difficult times, conditions, and circumstances well beyond the reach of their finite minds. What they had heard and witnessed was compelling. Their guiding light and words of wisdom, faith and comfort was the Holy Bible. Pilgrims put together the first contract on these shores for the glory of God. They had left the domain of Great Britain escaping the oppressive powers of the state church. In this hemisphere, there was not to be a King ruling the nation but a government of the people, by the people, for the people a democracy where the majority rule. The King may be replaced with an overbearing overextending, out of control government who do end-runs around the people in order to avoid the will of the people. They know that things like same sex marriage is not likely to meet the approval of the majority, so they make sure it ends up with the supreme court. All that is needed is 5 conscienceless judges who tease the constitution and have it say whatever is in the wind and as a mocking bird they write whatever they want the constitution to say. The source for guidance, wisdom, creativity, power to organize and direct in a positive way and bring people together was the Word of God . The constitution didn't make wisemen, but wise men wrote the constitution. Without the wisdom of God, we will perish. It's ironic that Madelyn O'hara's son became a minister of the gospel. God always wins. Church and State points people to the foundation that undergirds our freedom and posterity. If we fall on this rock, we will be broken; If this rock falls on us, we'll be ground to powder.

COMENTARY FROM FACEBOOK BY DR. SWEATTE

SAVE AMERICA OR THE AMERICA YOU HAVE KNOWN ALL YOUR LIFE IF YOU ARE BORN IN THIS COUNTRY WILL BECOME A DISMAL FOREST. ANTICHRIST DEMOCRATS HAVE A POLICY OR POLICIES THAT WILL DESTROY US. Democrats don't want borders. They think they can manipulate the system to have non citizens voting democrat . WE THE PEOPLE MUST RISE UP AGAINST THIS PLOT. Spanish speaking people whom are fleeing socialism and communism don't want to end up under socialism and communism again. YOU WANT TO BE FREE. Voting democrat will put chains on your feet. ONLY CHRISTIAN VALUES CAN GIVE YOU FREEDOM. SOLO LA VERDAD PUEDE HACERTE LIBRE

VOTER REGISTRATION WITH GOD

BEST TO BE AN EDUCATED VOTER

America: Democracy or Representative Republic is owned by "The People" However, People don't know what's right and what's left. Voters who are not informed vote on emotion and not from knowledge. Voting on the basis of morals and values is paramount. Morals are needed everywhere. Even in the home morals are needed with family "mom and dad" and every facet of life , business, relation in the work place, in government, and even in the church, people have forgotten the "golden rule" 'Do unto others as you would have them do to you". Since we have the Bible more than 150 years before we got a constitution, it only stands to reason that biblical values and principles present with the Pilgrims all the way from Great Brittan who signed the first contract on these shores to the glory of God should prevail. The rest is history these morals, principles and values permeated the culture and proved to be the best decision on earth. Power of the kingdom of God would prevail over every enemy to righteousness. The kingdom of God would offer mankind a way to brotherhood. As it has been throughout history, Satan has corrupted the mind of many and turned them away from the kingdom of God. God always found agents to lighten the path to freedom. Leaders such as Harriet Tubman,

Crispus Attucks, George Washington Carver, Thurgood Marshall, Dr. Martin Luther King Jr. and many many others. Most, if not all of these great leaders ascribed to Christian doctrine and biblical principles in spite of hell and works of the flesh. Flesh kills but the Spirit makes alive. (2 Cor. 3:6, Romans . It's these core values that hold fast basic tenets of faith and good will. By the grace of God, African Americans have carried the cross in many ways in America keeping her cognizant of the call to make one nation under God. These great leaders realized something far deeper than the color of the skin. They extrapolated far beyond the intangibles and broke   1 all physical limits for if God be for us "America", He is more than the world against us: Romans 8:31

COMMENTARY FOR THE NOW

SLAVERY THE WORST COMMENTARY ON AMERICAN LIFE:

As it was with joseph, where the intent of his brothers was evil, but God meant it for good. There is no point in looking back at ground already plowed, get busy planting seed for your upcoming harvest. It matters not now What are factors that come in to play regarding race and racism? "There are many factors!"

1. Societal norms: where racism is entrenched as normal, ordinary and acceptable, is so possibly because no one has challenged the system.

2. Lack of association: This is where an individual simply is turned off any time he/she sees a person of color: first, there is ignorance because the feeling is reciprocal. Overcome this dilemma by looking for good In each other, someone had to look for good in you. It helps when children are raised in the same community, go to the same church and school then the unknown becomes known and parents treats the other child just as another child.

3. Racial prejudice and behavior is learned. Children may be told not to play together but the benefit gained from relationship encourages the child to override the parents' objection

TEACHING CRITICAL RACE OR THAT RACE IS CRITICAL IS DIABOLICAL

ONE RACE, "THE HUMAN RACE"

This statement was never more true than realized by Appolles Sweatte in 1956 when he attended Sophia High School, Sophia West Virginia. Appolles was the first African American to attend an all white high school in West Virginia. Appolles was the only African American on the bus and in the school. Why switch from Stratton High an all African American High School in Beckley W.Va to Sophia? Stratton was some 8 miles from the Pemberton home while Sophia was 2 to 3 miles from Pemberton. However, there was a far greater cause to embrace than the distance to the schools, it was the distance to the White House. Conversations would go like this: "do you think an African American will ever become President? The answer was a resounding no. Friends Appolles played with every day were white and /or Italian. Their parents would tell them: "You can be raised in a coal mining camp and still become President". Neither Appolles nor his parents could see that ever happening with an African American.

COLOR! NUMBERS!, & STEREOTYPE

Free labor was no doubt the driving force behind confinement and servitude. Slaves were out numbered, easily identified, and considered inferior. The owners were enjoying free labor and were not interested in any advancement of the black race. Conditioning and inspiration of the black race would come from God. They would find solace and peace in spiritual songs. The double edged sword cut on both sides: slaves although suffering, were learning valuable skills. The grace of God was seen as provisions were made for Harriet Tubman to operate an underground railroad. This task was daring, eventful and dangerous. No one could hide her from the enemy but God. No one could give her the courage but God. Indelible in the writing of this story is the finger of God. What is permanent and everlasting is the plan of God not the will of man. For only God can bring out of conquest progress. The white race would not be able to hold the black race captive any longer than

God would allow. Weeping may endure for a night, but joy comes in the morning. The leadership of George Washington Carver, Fredrick Douglas, the brave soldiers and the black pilots who fought America's wars relentlessly with courage and love of country. The profound hatred bound in the heart of white men was deeper than just racism it was satanic, the roots of original sin the kind that made Cain kill his brother. Progress made in this country toward desegregation and unity and moving toward ONE NATION UNDER GOD has come because of the WORD of GOD. God's grace has given us men and   women of faith on both sides to follow mandates and dictates of faith taught in the bible. Consequently we have the greatest constitution ever written by laws of nature, inspired by nature's God.

On May 17, 1954, the U.S. Supreme Court outlawed racial segregation in public schools.

The ruling, ending the five-year case of Oliver Brown v. Board of Education of Topeka, Kansas, was a unanimous decision. ... Brown ruled that racial segregation itself was unconstitutional.

This was a step in the right direction. Positive change would be realized. Nine justices agreed unanimously to end segregation in public schools and other venues. In 1956 Appolles was invited by a playmate and best friend to attend Sophia High School with him. Being prone to accepting good challenges, Appolles considered this challenge a good one. Of course there was the opposition friends who warned of the danger. However, Appolles' parents who were people of faith stood by what they taught. We did have interracial worship and we lived in mixed communities in the little coal mining camp of Pemberton, West Virginia. Occasionally the "N" word came out and there was immediate retaliation. This had no bearing on the love for sports. Everybody joined together at the base ball diamond for the favorite past time baseball

THE TIME IS NOW

Nine justices would have to live with their decision. It took courage for these justices to face their constituency some which were blatantly opposed to integration. The problem was ameliorated to some degree by factors:

1.   Workers all did the same job (coal mining).

2.   All men got black every day in the coal mines

3.   They lived together in the community.

4.   Yes, there was segregation and occasional racial tension at times even against the Italians. However, there was a basis for reasoning. Many things we did together as God fearing people recognized other God fearing people

The Sweatte family lived on a farm of several acres. Most of the food was raised on the farm. There were poor white people who came to the Sweatte family for food. No one was turned away. You won't find this story in the media because it's good news. You will never make all people love you or even like you but you can demand respect. To keep trying to push the envelope for racism is foolish only God can give you true love. Progress made in our society regarding race relations is the result of the God kind of love.

GOD'S WISDOM INTERVENES

One day in the classroom one boy thought he would offend Appolles or embarrass him and get him upset. The young man raised is hand to ask a question. The question would have nothing to do with the class. His question went like this: "Isn't there a place out here called nigger tree county?? Appolles thought it was the funniest thing he had ever heard so, he's laughing like crazy the whole class is laughing with Appolles including the Teacher. Never heard such a wise crack in class again. A good laugh is better than anger. His statement defined him and demonstrated what he had learned, Since behavior is learned, the young man had learned to disrespect or dishonor people who was not of his race. This was one boy in a class of approximately 20 students. He thought he should use instructional time to find a way to use the N word. He didn't surprise anybody just demonstrated his ignorance. This behavior is typical of a small group that must be ignored. Don't give them support who are buried in deep race hatred.

Join the nine justices who put away the race card as much as possible and stepped forward to lead the country in a unified fashion. One Nation Under God. The ratio of 1 to 20 may be typical throughout the country. Accordingly 20% of Americans across the country applaud the progress made in race relations. The election of Barack Obama to the highest office in the Nation speaks volumes to the new age in America. Civil Rights laws protect the interest of every citizen. Organizations like BLM and CRT (Critical race jargon) are senseless, counterproductive and unamerican. Many Whites are asking: "what can we do to correct the injustices portrayed on the American blacks? The answer is "NOTHING". Just treat every citizen the same. Do what Jesus taught especially if you claim Christianity. Follow the lead of the founding fathers. What should black Americans do?

1. Take your rightful place in society: (think like an owner) This land is your land.

2. Don't let others define you

3. Accept your identity, work to improve and achieve high goals

4. Think smart; make wise choices

5. The constitution defends Americans think AMERICAN

6. Avoid race sensitive jargon. Opinions are worth what you have in your pockets. Your negative opinion is worth the two cents you have in your pocket.

7. Train in fields that guarantee pay

8. Have faith in God

9. Embrace morality

10. Forgive those dead white folks who mistreated your great, great, great grand parents 100 years ago. Anger and fears are enemies to faith

11. Set meaningful goals. Visualize your future. How do you see yourself in one year, in two years, in five years, in fifteen years.

12. Do you have a plan? Are you working your plan?

13. Develop a prayer life

14. Be more God conscious and less world conscious.

15. If you have faith you can say to the mountain: "Be removed" and it will obey you. Mark 11:22

16. Your country can only exist and enjoy the successes of the past if we accentuate the values of the founding fathers

NOT OF THIS WORLD

Being a Christian Nation has very little to do with the constitution in that Christianity has not derived impetus from the constitution but rather the constitution derived its foundational principles, precepts, and concepts, traditions and customs, education and practices are from Judeo-Christian values. Christianity is not of this world and is ordered by a far greater authority. The word "Christian" in the article above refers to an individual or group who ascribe to a specific philosophy, doctrine or denomination under the umbrella recognized as Christian. The constitution operates horizontally not vertically. The caliber and quality of men hammering out rules and regulation governing society, institutions, families, cities, states and behavior ought to be men of conscience. Men of conscience arguing for the formation of the constitution in its origin and infancy, were by and large men who derived their consciousness from Judeo-Christian values. "God was in Christ reconciling the world to Himself". 2 Cor. 5:19 Therefore be reconciled to God by receiving His Holy Spirit in Jesus Christ. Then you will be able to love everybody.

5 main systems of government throughout the known world.

Understanding different political systems is important. Each political system has its advantages and disadvantages. it is worth considering . the merits of other political systems, and perhaps incorporating some of the ideas into your own system.

 Democracy - A democracy in a more traditional sense is a political system that allows for each individual to participate. There are two rather popular democracies :

c.) Direct Democracy: Many scholars point to Athens as an example of direct democracy. Technically, every citizen has an equal say in the workings of government. (The qualifications for being considered a citizen are completely different.) Citizens could show up at a meeting, and then directly participate in the governing process, and the process of making laws.

- Representative Democracy: in a representative democracy set-up, citizens elect representatives who actually make the law, The United States operates similarly to this principle. Citizens elect legislators who, in turn, make laws. In the U.S., even the president isn't elected directly; representatives called electors make the decision (although designated electors usually vote   according to the wishes of the citizens in their states) Other types of democracies where citizens are more directly involved in polity making and in making laws include Deliberative Democracy   Democratic Socialism. Policies made or laws passed are generally socialistic in nature.

Public: In theory, a democratic republic is a political system in which the government remains mostly subject to those governed. Some scholars define any political system in which the citizens legitimize the government. As such:

Monarchy: When most of us think of a monarchy, we think of the political systems of medieval European countries. In a monarchy, a ruler is not usually chosen by the voice of the people or their representatives. Often a monarch is the head of state until he or she abdicates or until death. In many cases a monarch is the final word in government. Monarchy may be placed in three camps: absolute, elective or non sovereign monarchy. Communism: in most cases, a communist state is based on the ideology of communism as taught by Marx and/or Lenin. However, some argue that these political systems are not true to the ideals espoused by these revolutionary thinkers. Communist states are often dominated by a single party, or a group of people. A planned economy is often part of the governing class, and in many cases resources are taken and then redistributed to others.

CHURCH GOVERNMENT: CHAPTER I

Church government (or church polity) is that branch of ecclesiology(study of the . church) that addresses the organizational structure and hierarchy of the church. There are basically three types of church government that have developed in the va pious Christian denominations: the episcopal, the Presbyterian, and the congregational.

The episcopal form of government has been the polity of the Catholic Church as early as Ignatius of' Antioch, all the way' down to the time of the Reformation. Advocates for an episcopal form of church government argue that the sheer fact that it went virtually uncontested until the time of the Reformation testifies to its claims of apostolicity, although not all contemporary episcopalian apologists argue from history rather than Scripture, A notable example is Ray Sutton, the Suffragan Bishop in the Diocese of Mid-America of the Reformed Episcopal Church, who has produced work arguing that the episcopal system is biblical.

Presbyterian and Reformed Churches

Typically, original authority--that is the authority that the church believes Christ gave to it--is said to reside at the local elder level in this model of polity. Thus the "highest" authority in a Presbyterian or reformed church (after Christ) is said to be the Elders of the church. Those elders are typically elected by the congregation on a periodic basis (usually a terns lasts about 3 years). Sometimes elders are elected by the drawing of lots, congregational polity as follows:

"The oxford Dictionary of the Christian Church defines congregationalism" as "that form of Church polity which rests on the

independence and autonomy of each local church." According to this source, the principles of democracy in church government rest on the belief that Christ is the sole head of his church, the members are all priests unto God, and these units are regarded each as an outcrop and representative of the church universal." (Who Runs the Church)? :

FORMATION OF AMERICAN GOVERNMENT CH3

it was actually in the drafting of these state constitutions that the revolution was accomplished, Naturally, the first object of the framers was to secure those "unalienable rights," the violation of 'which had caused them to repudiate their connection with England

» Indeed Consequently, each constitution began with a declaration or bill of rights, and Virginia ' s, which served as a model for all the others, included a declaration of principles such as popular sovereignty, rotation in office, freedom of elections, and an enumeration of the fundamental liberties moderate bail and humane punishments, a militia instead of a standing army, speedy trials by the law of the land, trial by jury. Godless men tear at the foundation and reduce what was designed for life, liberty and the pursuit of happiness to rubbish and chaos. Without a strong vertical relationship, everything will be out of balance and open to the enemy. Don't kid yourself we've come this far by faith leaning on the

Lord. Rest assured, the further we get away from the laws of God and biblical principles, the closer we are to destruction. "<u>Stands to Reason</u>" Internet <u>A Two Sided Coin</u>

We can safely draw two conclusions from these facts which serve to inform our understanding of the relationship between religion and government in the U.S. First, Christianity was the prevailing moral and intellectual influence shaping the nation from the outset. Christian influence was pervasive in all aspects of American life from education to politics. Theodore the present concept of a rigid wall of separation hardly seems historically justified. Virtually everyone of the founders saw a vital link between civil religion and civil government. George Washington's admonition in his farewell speech September 19, 1796 were: " Of all the dispositions and habits which lead to political prosperity, religion and morality are indispensable supports; And let us indulge with caution the supposition that morality can be maintained without religion. Reason and experience both forbid us to expect that national morality can prevail in exclusion of religious principles". <u>The Annals of America</u> (Chicago Encyclopedia Britannica 1976).

Secondly, The founders stopped short of giving their Christian religion a position of legal privilege in the tradition of the early church, believers were to be salt and light. The first amendment insured the liberty needed for Christianity to be a preserving influence and a moral beacon but it also insured Christianity would never be the law of the land. Christianity cannot be legislated. Laws do not make Christians. Christian values are derived from the Holy Scriptures and the guiding light of the Holy Spirit produces exceptional quality of life and builds a moral conviction as demonstrated by the "work ethic".

The founders that produced the constitution and the participating constituency that implemented practices and lived out their lives under the prevailing moral code, were by and large Christian. It stands to reason that if Christianity distinguishes America from the rest of the world, and when 6 America becomes the leading country in the world, whose greatest leaders came from Christian Institutions, Universities, Schools, Churches and societies, then it seem grossly repugnant that the country would want to rid itself of its core support system. The answer is found in the parable of the wheat and tares: (Mathew 13:24-30). While we quietly closed the bible and looked solely to the wind of science for instruction and direction we forgot that science as a Confederation was not working. America needed a new form of government. It had to be strong enough to maintain national unity over a large geographic area, but not so strong as to become a tyranny. Unable to find an exact model in history to fit America's unique situation, delegates met at Philadelphia in 1787 to create their own solution to the problem. Their creation was the United States Constitution.

<u>The Pledge of Allegiance</u> (1892) According to its author, utopian novelist Francis Bellamy. This well-known oath "began as an intensive communing with...our national history, from the Declaration of Independence onwards..." It has been the subject of controversy for more than a century. 1892, Francis Bellamy wrote and published the first Pledge of Allegiance in his magazine, Youth's Companion. It was publicly recited for the first . time at the first Columbus Day celebration, held that year. [1] Bellamy's first pledge read: "I pledge allegiance to my flag and to the Republic for which it stands; one nation, indivisible, with liberty and justice for all "[2] The pledge soon became popular and was adopted by schools across the nation.

By the time of the Second World War, many states had made the daily recitation of the pledge mandatory for teachers and students. This led to a controversy about the pledge. In 1940, with the threat of war hanging over the nation, a case went to the U.S. Supreme Court challenging the mandatory pledge law in West Virginia. There, several students refused to recite the pledge on religious grounds. Their parents claimed the law

- violated the Constitution. The court upheld the law, finding that the state's goal to instill national unity and patriotism should not be overruled by the judiciary unless it significantly affected religious rights. [3]

Three years later, the disputed West Virginia flag salute law came again before the court. This time the court held that no person should be compelled to state beliefs which violated personal conscience or conviction and that while the state could require the pledge, a pupil could not be punished for refusing to say it. [4]

In the 1950s with America embroiled in the Cold War with the Soviet Union, a change was made to the pledge. Wishing to emphasize the philosophical differences between the United States and the communist world, Congress passed a law in 1954, inserting the words "under God" into the pledge. It then read:,.
allegiance to the flag of the United States of America and to the republic for which it stands. one nation, under God, indivisible. with liberty and justice for all."

During the turmoil of the 1960s new challenges faced the pledge. Students protesting U.S. involvement in Vietnam and issues of inequality at home often refused to salute the flag. This prompted a proposed new version of the pledge. At the invitation of Look magazine, James Allen, a former U.S. Commissioner of Education, revised the pledge to meet these concerns. His 1970 version read: "I pledge allegiance to the flag of the United States of America and dedicate myself to the principle that the republic for which it stands shall be in truth one Nation, under God, indivisible, . dedicated to liberty and justice for all.

I." Allen hoped that by emphasizing the ideals of America and acknowledging that all citizens had not yet achieved them would help revive the pledge. [5] In 2002, a new controversy surrounded the pledge. An Oregon man who was an atheist, filed suit in federal court on behalf of his child, a public school student. The suit claimed that the classroom recitation of the pledge violated the establishment clause of the First Amendment and constituted a overnmental endorsement of religion.

(Newdow v. United States Congress) The Ninth Circuit Court of Appeals agreed. Its opinion found the phrase "under God" was not merely a passive reference to religion. It also found that schools should not endorse the concept that our country was "under God" by allowing the pledge in classrooms or school events. A storm of protest greeted the court's decision and the judge stayed, or postponed, his order to ban the pledge until the decision could be judicially reviewed.[6]

For 120 years, Americans have recited and debated the pledge of allegiance. It remains to be seen whether or not the courts will overturn the Newdow decision, but it is clear that the pledge remains with us as we move into the 21st century. Who were these men who were involved in establishing the framework for the constitution? What were their beliefs? Facts are recorded, school texts abound with reference to our religious heritage. Entire organizations are dedicated to returning America to her spiritual roots. We are in the year of our Lord 2015 A.D. 228 years since 81 year old Benjamin Franklin on June28, 1787, . prayed an emotional prayer calling men to humility. That was the turning point of a hopelessly stalled convention. James Madison . recorded the event in his collection of notes and debates from the Federal Convention. We are able to see and recognize the Holy Spirit at work as God the final authority inspired Benjamin Franklin, a deist, to ask for grace to help during the time of a deadlocked convention. What religions were present and participated in the constitutional convention? Certainly there were godless men among the early leaders of our nation, though some of those cited as examples of founding fathers turn out to be insignificant players.

For example Thomas Paine and Ethan Allen may have been hostile to Evangelical Christianity, but they were firebrands of the Revolution, not intellectual architects of the constitution. Paine didn't arrive in this country until 1774 and only stayed a short time. As for the others, George Washington, Samuel Adams, James Madison, John Witherspoon, Alexander Hamilton, John Jay, John Adams, Patrick Henry, and even Thomas Jefferson. Their personal correspondence, biographies and public statements are replete with quotations showing that these thinkers had political philosophies deeply influenced by Christianity. Founding fathers refers to a specific group of men. The 55 delegates to the constitutional convention were accompanied by other important players not in attendance, like Jefferson whose thinking deeply influenced the shaping of our nation. These 55 founding fathers make up the core. The denominational affiliation of these men were a matter of public record.

Among the delegates were 28 Episcopalians, 8 Presbyterians 7 Congregationalist, 2 Lutheran 2 Dutch Reformed, 2 Methodist, 2 Roman Catholics, 1 unknown, and 3 Deist Williamson, Wilson This is a revealing tally. It shows that the members of the constitutional convention, the most influential group of men Shapira the political foundation of our nation were almost all Christian.51 c a full 93% indeed. 70% were Calvinist, the others Episcopalians, Presbyterians, and Dutch Reformed, were considered by some to the most extreme and dogmatic form of Christianity. The wisdom (God is seen jn the design and architecture in setting forth guidelines consistent with the distinctive relationship between God and His creation. For a moment we must step back and ask the question: "what is God doing? What is He calling for in this construction? WI will the finished product look like? Just as sure as you are born, a: God gave Moses absolute minute detailed instructions regarding to development of the tabernacle,(Exodus chapters 25 thru 40), divers revelation and inspiration is at work in the framework of the constitution. What we see in the foundation and architecture of America is dynamics of the church age. implemented by the overshadowing watchful eye of the Holy Spirit. In Exodus 25, God Moses to have the Israelites bring the finest materials: fine, linen, spices, silver, gold, oil, onyx stones etc. build the tabernacle according to all that was shown in the mount. We are in the church age where Jesus said: on this rock" (referring to the revelation received by Peter which enabled him to identify Jesus Christ as the Son of God), I will build my church, and the gates of hell will not   prevail against it. The church represents the body of Christ. All people, races, tongues, nationalities, religions, those who agree, those who disagree, all are invited to enjoy the blessings of the of true God and the only savior of the world Jesus Christ. Of course Jesus Christ stands out in history as the only Savior who came to the world and made the statement that he came to die for the sins of world. He announced that he would die at the hands of evil men.

OFFICER OF THE U. S. CONSTITUTION; GOVERNOR OF MASSACHUSETTS 1 . . . [rely] upon the merits of Jesus Christ for a pardon of all my sins. The name of the Lord (says the Scripture) is a strong tower; thither the righteous flee and are safe [Proverbs 18:10]. Let us secure His favor and He will lead us through the journey of this life and at length receive us to a better place. conceive we cannot better express ourselves than by humbly supplicating the Supreme Ruler of the world . . . that the confusions that are and have been among the nations may be overruled by the promoting and speedily bringing in the holy and happy period when the kingdoms of our Lord and Savior Jesus Christ may be everywhere established, and the people willingly bow to the scepter of Him who is the Prince of Peace. He also called on the State of Massachusetts to pray that . . .the peaceful and glorious reign of our Divine Redeemer may be known and enjoyed throughout the whole family of mankind. [12] we may with one heart and voice humbly implore His gracious and free pardon through Jesus Christ, supplicating His Divine aid . . . [and] above all to cause the religion of Jesus Christ, in its true spirit, to spread far and wide till the whole earth shall be filled with His glory. [-with true contrition of heart to confess their sins to God and implore forgiveness through the merits and mediation of Jesus Christ our Savior

MILITARY OFFICER; SIGNER OF THE DECLARATION OF INDEPENDENCE; JUDGE; GOVERNOR OF NEW HAMPSHIRE: Called on the people of New Hampshire .. to confess before God their aggravated transgressions and to implore His pardon and forgiveness through the merits and mediation of Jesus Christ . . . [t]hat the knowledge of the Gospel of Jesus Christ may be made known to all nations, pure and undefiled religion universally prevail, and the earth be fill with the glory of the Lord Gunning Bedford

MILITARY OFFICER; MEMBER OF THE CONTINE-NTAL CONGRESS; SIGNER OF THE CONSTITUTION•, FEDERAL JUDGE To the triune God - the Father, the Son, and the Holy Ghost - be ascribed all honor and dominion, forevermore - Amen. [Lé]

Elias Boudinot

PRESIDENT OF CONGRESS; SIGNED THE PEACE TREATY TO END THE AMERICAN REVOLUTION•, FIRST ATTORNEY ADMITTED -TO THE U. S. SUPREME COURT BAR; FRAMER OF THE BILL OF RIGHTS; DIRECTOR OF THE U. S. MINT

Let us enter on this important business under the idea that we are Christians on whom the eyes of the world are now turned... [L]et us earnestly call and beseech Him, for Christ's sake, to preside in our councils We can only depend on the all powerful influence of the Spirit of God, Whose Divine aid and assistance it becomes us as a Christian people most devoutly to implore. Therefore I move that some minister of the Gospel be requested to attend this Congress every morning . in order to open the meeting with prayer. A CLOUD OF WITNESSES SAY THIS NATION WAS BORN OUT OF CHRISTIAN THOUGHT,

PHILOSOPHY AND DOCTRINE. ALTHOUGH TARES HAVE GROWN UP WITH THEM, "WHEAT" IS THE PREFERRED PRODUCT, NOT "TARES." IF GOD WILLS, THE SALT WILL REDISCOVER IT'S SALTINESS AND THIS CHRISTIAN NATION WILL RISE TO ITS RIGHTFUL PLACE OF DOMINANCE.

SEPARATION OF CHURCH AND STATE??? Our Founding Fathers set this great nation of ours upon the twin towers of religion and morality. Our first president, George Washington, said that anyone who would attack these twin towers could not possibly consider themselves to be a loyal American. Not only did they set us up as a nation under God, but a nation founded upon the Judaic-Christian principles summarized in the words, "The laws of nature and the laws of nature's God," words that we find in the Declaration of Independence.

Never Intended to Separate State from God or from Religion or from Prayer The First Amendment never intended to separate Christian principles from government. yet today we so often hear the First Amendment couples with the phrase "separation of church and state." The First Amendment simply states: "Congress shall make no law respecting an establishment of religion or prohibiting the free exercise thereof."

Obviously, the words "separation," "church," or "state" are not found in the First Amendment; furthermore, that phrase appears in no founding document. While most recognize the phrase "separation of church and state," few know its source; but it is important to understand the origins of that phrase. What is the history of the First Amendment?

The process of drafting the First Amendment made the intent of the Founders abundantly clear; for before they approved the final wording, the First Amendment went through nearly a dozen different iterations and extensive discussions. Those discussions—recorded in the Congressional Records from June 7 through September 25 of 1789—make clear their intent for the First Amendment. By it, the Founders were saying: "We do not want in America what we had in Great Britain: we don't want one denomination running the nation. We will not all be Catholics, or Anglicans, or any other single denomination. We do want God's principles, but we don't want one denomination running the nation. '

This intent was well understood, as evidenced by court rulings after the First Amendment. For example, a 1799 court declared:

"By our form of government, the Christian religion is the established religion; and all sects and denominations of Christians are placed on the same equal footing."

Again, note the emphasis: "We do want Christian principles—we do want God's principles—but we don't want one denomination to run the nation. "

By Fr. Bill McCarthy MSA

Regardless where people come from, all recognize America as a Christian nation. Christianity is an extension of the Abrahamic Covenant in whose seed (which is Jesus Christ), all nations on earth are blessed. Christians see all nations, kindred, and tongues as people called of God to receive the fullness of the Abrahamic Covenant by accepting Jesus . Christ Savior of the world. Christians do not strap bombs about their bodies and kill hundreds of people as an act to be rewarded by their . god. Quiet to the contrary, Jesus Christ loved us and died in our place. His blood reaches every living human creature with forgiveness for the asking. There is only one Jesus, only one cross where He died, and He is the only one that rose from the dead and gave us the gospel of love. You are the one who should receive Him and be free.

Mature Christians understand how to love even their enemies. The Christian community feed more people throughout the world than any other religion. No one's life is threatened in order to force them to become Christian. Christian giving demonstrates the love of God.

A CHRISTIAN NATION OVERRUN BY ANTICHRIST and DOCTRINES OF DEVILS

Rev. William Owens, President and Founder of the Coalition of African American Pastors was very vocal in opposition to "same sex marriage" PUBLISHED JULY 31, 2012 ON YOUTUBE. COALITION OF 3742 PASTORS invited President Obama for conference and was ignored Published on Nov 13, 2012 ON YOUTUBE

Surprisingly, Bishop T.D. Jakes has not publicly come out against Barrack Hussein Obama and his support for same-sex marriage. According to the

Article, Bishop Jakes, Founder and Pastor of the Potters House in Texas and presumed Advisor of the President, has not publicly denounced same sex marriage. The writer contends that Bishop Jakes is for same sex marriage & the fruit of his stance has brought forth rotten fruit. (Statement comes from special report on You tube) Bishop T.D. Jakes speaks for himself. His position is important. Statement from the Bishop in support of the Biblical mandate that marriage can only be valid when engaged by one man and one woman; And that any other union cannot be considered marriage, is important.

It is noteworthy that the issue with same sex marriage was boiling over even in 2012. I am happy to point out that not all African American Pastors drank the Obama cool-aid. Many Pastors remain dedicated to God and Family and Country.

There are two deceptive statements that poison the mind and forms this Anti-Christ, Anti-American thought which opens the gateway to corruption. (1) Satan's plan to break up the family, (2) Corrupt Schools with Anti-Christ philosophy (3) Demoralize Society, as Administrations dance with the devil, and fail to represent examples of quality, dignity, and respect.

1. THIS IS NOT A CHRISTIAN NATION
2. SEPARATION OF CHURCH AND STATE
3. THESE TWO STATEMENTS ARE USED

INDISCRIMINATELY TO JUSTIFY REJECTION OF BIBLICAL TEACHING and ORACLES OF LIFE NOT A CHRISTIAN NATION???

Thought precedes action. What was the prevailing thought of the Pilgrims? What persistent thought prevailed in the formation of family, business, churches, institutions especially Government. What thought was pervasive in the work ethic? Was it not religious thought? Was it not Judeo-Christian? It was not Islam, or Buda, or Confucius or Pagan, it was Christian. What thought prevailed in the formation of the Constitution? Testimony of the Founding Fathers WHAT DID SIGNERS OF THE DECLA-RATION OF INDEPENDENCE SAY?

John Adams

 SIGNER OF THE DECLARATION OF INDEPENDENCE; JUDGE; DIPLOMAT; ONE OF TWO SIGNERS OF THE BILL OF RIGHTS; SECOND

PRESIDENT OF THE UNITED STATES . SIGNER OF THE DECLARATION OF INDEPENDENCE; JUDGE; DIPLOMAT; ONE OF TWO SIGNERS OF THE BILL OF RIGHTS; SECOND PRESIDENT OF THE UNITED STATES . The general principles on which the fathers achieved independence were the general principles of Christianity. I will avow that I then believed, and now . believe, that those general principles of Christianity are as eternal and immutable as the existence and attributes of God.

Without religion, this world would be something not fit to be mentioned in polite company: I mean hell! The Christian religion is, above all the religions that ever prevailed or existed in ancient or modern times, the religion of wisdom, virtue, equity and humanity.2Suppose a nation in some distant region should take the Bible for their only law book and every member should regulate his conduct by the precepts there exhibited. . . . What a Eutopia — what a Paradise would this region be! 41 have examined all religions, and the result is that the Bible is the best book in the world.

John Quincy Adams

SIXTH PRESIDENT OF THE UNITED STATES; DIPLOMAT; SECRETARY OF STATE; U. S. SENATOR; U. S. REPRESENTATIVE;

"OLD MAN ELOQUENT"; "HELL-HOUND OF ABOLITION" My hopes of a future life are all founded upon the Gospel of Christ and I cannot cavil or quibble away [evade or object to]. the whole tenor of His conduct by which He sometimes positively asserted and at others countenances [permits] His disciples in asserting that He was God. The hope of a Christian is inseparable from his faith. Whoever believes in the Divine inspiration of the Holy Scriptures must hope that the religion of Jesus shall prevail throughout the earth. Never since the foundation of the world have the prospects of mankind been more encouraging to that hope than they appear to be at the present time. And may the associated distribution of the Bible proceed and prosper till the Lord shall have made "bare His holy arm in the eyes of all the nations, and all the ends of the earth shall see the salvation of our God" [Isaiah 52: 10]. ᶻIn the chain of human events, the birthday of the nation is indissolubly linked with the birthday of the Savior. The Declaration of Independence laid the cornerstone of human government upon the first precepts of Christianity.

Samuel Adams

SIGNER OF THE DECLARATION OF INDEPENDENCE; "FATHER OF THE AMERICAN REVOLUTION"; RATIFIER OF THE U. S.

CONSTITUTION; GOVERNOR OF MASSACHUSETTS

I . . .[rely] upon the merits of Jesus Christ for a pardon of all my sins.

The name of the Lord (says the Scripture) is a strong tower; thither the righteous flee and are safe [Proverbs 18:10]. Let us secure His favor and He will lead us through the journey of this life and at length receive us to a better. I conceive we cannot better express ourselves than by humbly supplicating the Supreme Ruler of the world . . . that the confusions that are and have been among the nations may be overruled by the promoting and speedily bringing in the holy and happy period when the kingdoms of our Lord and Savior Jesus Christ may be everywhere established, and the people willingly bow to the scepter of Him who is the Prince of Peace. He also called on the State of Massachusetts to pray that . . .the peaceful and glorious reign of our divine Redeemer may be known and enjoyed throughout the whole family of mankind. we may with one heart and voice humbly implore His gracious and free pardon through Jesus Christ, supplicating His Divine aid ... [and] above all to cause the religion of Jesus Christ, in its true spirit, to spread far and wide till the whole earth shall be filled with His glory. with true contrition of heart to confess their sins to God and implore forgiveness through the merits and mediation of Jesus Christ our Savior.

MILITARY OFFICER; SIGNER OF THE DECLARATION OF INDEPENDENCE; JUDGE; GOVERNOR OF NEW HAMPSHIRE

Called on the people of New Hampshire . .. to confess before God their aggravated transgressions and to implore His pardon and forgiveness through the merits and mediation of Jesus Christ ... that the knowledge of the Gospel of Jesus Christ may be made known to all nations, pure and undefiled religion universally prevail, and the earth be fill with the glory of the Lord.

Gunning Bedford

MILITARY OFFICER; MEMBER OF THE CONTINENTAL CONGRESS; SIGNER OF THE CONSTITUTION; FEDERAL.

JUDGE

To the triune God - the Father, the Son, and the Holy Ghost - be ascribed all honor and dominion, forevermore- Amen. 1&

Elias Boudinot

PRESIDENT OF CONGRESS; SIGNED THE PEACE TREATY TO END THE AMERICAN REVOLUTION; FIRST ATTORNEY
ADMITTED TO THE U. S. SUPREME COURT BAR;; FRAMER OF THE BILL OF RIGHTS; DIRECTOR OF THE U. S.

MINT. Let us enter on this important business under the idea that we are Christians on whom the eyes of the world are now turned ... Let us earnestly call and beseech Him, for Christ's sake, to preside in our councils .... We can only depend on the all powerful influence of the Spirit of God, Whose Divine aid and assistance it becomes us as a Christian people most devoutly to implore. Therefore I move that some minister of the Gospel be requested to attend this Congress every morning ... in order to open the meeting with prayer.

John Adams

SIGNER OF THE DECLARATION OF INDEPENDENCE; JUDGE; DIPLOMAT; ONE OF TWO SIGNERS OF THE BILL OF RIGHTS; SECOND PRESIDENT OF THE UNITED STATES

The general principles on which the fathers achieved independence were the general principles of Christianity. I will avow that I then believed, and now believe, that those general principles of Christianity are as eternal and immutable as the existence and attributes of God.!

Without religion, this world would be something not fit to be mentioned in polite company: I mean hell.

The Christian religion is, above all the religions that ever prevailed or existed in ancient or modem times, the religion of wisdom, virtue, equity and humanity.~

John Adams and other framers of the constitution pointed out key founding virtues that are cohesive in the final draft of the constitution.

(1) Independence was achieved on the general principles of Christianity.

John Adams believed that those general principles of Christianity are as eternal and immutable as the existence and attributes of God

1.   Without religion this world would be hell.

2.   The Christian religion is, above all the religions that ever prevailed or existed in ancient or modern times, the religion of wisdom, virtue, equity and humanity

<u>John Adams</u>

George Washington and FAITH

By 1778, George Washington had so often **witness**

God's intervention that on August 20, he wrote Thomas Nelson that: "The Hand of providence has been so   conspicuous in all this, that he must be worse than an infidel that lacks faith, and more than wicked, that has not gratitude enough to acknowledge his obligations" James Adams:

Without religion, this world would be something not fit to be mentioned in polite company: I mean hell. The Christian religion is, above all the religions that ever prevailed or existed in ancient or modern times, the religion of wisdom, virtue, equity and humanity. The only "religion" contributing bountifully and extemporaneously, as though inspired to the progress and success of the United States is Christianity.

A CLOUD OF WITNESSES SAY THIS NATION WAS BORN OUT OF CHRISTIAN THOUGHT, PHILOSOPHY AND DOCTRINE.

ALTHOUGH TARES HAVE GROWN UP WITH THE WHEAT,

"WHEAT" IS THE PREFERRED PRODUCT, NOT "TARES." IF GOD WILLS, THE SALT WILL REDISCOVER IT'S SALTINESS AND THIS CHRISTIAN NATION WILL RISE TO ITS RIGHTFUL PLACE OF DOMINANCE.

SEPARATION OF CHURCH AND STATE???

Our Founding Fathers set this great nation of ours upon the twin towers of religion and morality. Our first president, George Washington, said that anyone who would attack thesc twin towers could not possibly consider themselves to be a loyal American. Not only did they set us up as a nation under God, but a nation founded upon the Judaic-Christian principles summarized in the words, "The laws of nature and the laws of nature's God," words that we find in the Declaration of Independence.

Never Intended to Separate State from God or from Religion or from Prayer

The First Amendment never intended to separate Christian principles from government. yet today we so often hear the First Amendment couples with the phrase "separation of church and state." The First Amendment simply states:

"Congress shall make no law respecting an establishment of religion or prohibiting the free exercise thereof. "

Obviously, the words "separation," "church," or "state" are not found in the First Amendment; furthermore, that phrase appears in no founding document . While most recognize the phrase "separation of church and state," few know its source; but it is important to understand the origins of that phrase. What is the history of the First Amendment? The process of drafting the First Amendment made the intent of the Founders abundantly clear; for before they approved the final wording, . the First Amendment went through nearly a dozen different iterations and extensive discussions, Those discussions— recorded in the Congressional Records from June 7 through September 25 of 1789—make clear their intent for the First Amendment. By it, the Founders were saying: "We do not want in America what we had in Great Britain: we don't want one denomination running the nation. We will not all be Catholics, or Anglicans, or any other single denomination. We do want God's principles, but we don't want one denomination running the nation. "

This intent was well understood, as evidenced by court rulings after the First Amendment. For example, a 1799 court declared:

"By our form of government, the Christian religion is the established religion; and all sects and denominations of Christians are placed on the same equal footing."

Again, note the emphasis: "We do want Christian principles— we do want God's principles—but we don't want one denomination to run the nation. " By Fr. Bill McCarthy MSA

Is the United States a "Christian nation"? Some Americans think

AMEFRICA A JUDEO-CHRISTIAN NATION

So. Religious Right activists and right-wing television preachers often claim that the United States was founded to be a Christian nation Even some politicians agree. If the people who make this assertion are merely saying that most Americans are Christians, they might have a point. But those who argue that America is a Christian nation usually mean something more, insisting that the country should be officially Christian. The very character of our country is at stake in the outcome of this debate.

NOT OF THIS WORLD

Being a Christian Nation has very little to do with the constitution in that Christianity has not derived impetus from the constitution but rather the Constitution derived its foundational principles, precepts and concepts, traditions and customs, education and practices are from Judeo-Christian values. Christianity is not of this world and is ordered by a far greater authority. The word Christian in the article above refers to an individual or group who ascribe to a specific philosophy, doctrine, or denomination under the umbrella recognized as Christian. The constitution operates horizontally not vertically. The caliber and quality of men hammering out rules and regulations governing society, institutions, families, cities, states and behavior ought to be men of conscience. Men of conscience arguing for the formation of the constitution in its origin and infancy, were by and large men who derived their consciousness from Judeo-Christian values.

IT'S CHRISTIAN BECAUSE YOUR FOUNDATION (IF YOU ARE AMERICAN), WAS ESTABLISHED BY BELIEVERS IN THE BIBLE AND CHRISTIANITY

The Biblical foundation, morals, values, and principles built the strongest most free nation in the world. HAS NOTHING TO DO WITH RELIGIOUS RIGHT OR TELEVANGELIST, BUT <u>TRUTH</u>

One pastor said: "the president was elected President not Pastor of the Country". If you are a real pastor, concerned about the future of the country you should point the President to the principles that made the country great as stated by the second President John Adams and all others with a few exceptions. If the President's programs and policies go counter to proven sound judgments, it is the Pastor's place to warn him as the voice of morality not to compromise and cow tow to the political correct jargon.

No true Christian whether President, Governor or Mayor will support the slaughter of unborn children and the marketing of their organs

No Christian President would stoop so low as to honor the most perverted diabolical ungodly act as men with men and women with women. This act poisons the environment, creates chaos for school children destroys family identity, stops reproduction. This very act comes from the pit of hell.

Christianity "(disciples of Christ)" is categorically and profoundly different from any other practice called RELIGION

a. Christianity is the only practice whose founder established his church by His resurrection from the dead. THE PROCLAMATION FROM THE EARLY FIRST CENTURY IS "HE'S ALIVE", HE'S ALIVE. YOU CAN HAVE A RELATIONSHIP WITH THE LIVING CHRIST.

(1) Christian values, principles, ethics and morals are woven into the fabric of traditional American culture. Dr. Martin Luther King Jr. drew from the bank of justice based on biblical doctrine and teachings. Biblical principles influenced the courts and all aspects of government.

GOVERNMENT WITHOUT GOD IS CHAOS

Separation of church and state clause from the supreme court ruling NEVER FOUND IN THE CONSTITUTION, WAS TO PREVENT A STATE RUN CHRISTIAN CHURCH. IT WAS NOT

TO STOP CHRISTIANITY AND NO OTHER RELIGION WAS EVEN INVOLVED. IT WAS NOT TO HAVE A STATE RUN

BAPTIST, METHODIST, PRESBYTERIAN, LUTHERAN, CATHOLIC, EPISCOPAL OR ANY OTHER CHRISTIAN DENOMINATION.

It was not to prohibit the free exercise of religious faith in the public square or to prohibit school from beginning with prayer as congress begins. This entire group was CHRISTIAN. Whether Baptist, Episcopalian, Catholic or Lutheran, these are all Christian. There was no other religion involved. The words "church" and /or "religion" referred to the Christian Faith only. The Christian Community did not object to the broad definition applied to "church" and "religion". The Church operated on the principle that in Christ, all nations are invited to receive eternal life through Jesus Christ. All other religions are to be subject to the Mother religion (Christianity) in the U.S. To allow any outsider to bring in some other doctrine to overrule in any way the tenets of the Christian way of life in its basic and fundamental purpose would be disastrous. The basic biblical doctrine of Christianity is "LOVE". Is it always practiced? No. Do we as a people ever break the law? Yes we do. The law is still right. We have to learn to conform to what we know is right. This Christian Nation did not reject other religions as long as they were law abiding citizens. They are even allowed to teach things contrary to Christianity. The principle of love remained the order of the day. Through love and fellowship everyone can come to know the truth and be free. Jesus said: "I am the way the truth and the life: No one can come to the Father except by me". Any religion that teaches hate, racism, violence, murder, oppression or disrespect in any form is not of God and is sensual, devilish, and destructive.

1. These principles and values influencing early life is the only real defense against wickedness violence, murder, immorality, ungodliness and all forces that are determined to bring the country down. The Christian message has

2. demonstrated its power to build strong families, business, churches, schools and communities. FORGET ABOUT DEMOCRAT and REBUPLICAN, VOTE FOR CONVICTIONS THAT ARE BASED ON THE VALUES OF THE FOUNDINGS FATHERS.

IF THE BIBLE RIGHTLY INTERPRETED DECLARES AN ACT WRONG, IT CANNOT BE MADE RIGHT BY THE SUPREME COURT. ANY CANDIDATE WHO DOES NOT RESPECT THE LAW OF NATURE'S GOD

DOES NOT DESERVE TO BE PRESIDENT OF THE UNITED STATES. This argument stands against the counterculture of today and the misguided predilections of the current administration.

SOCIAL EXPLOSION

SOCIAL ISSUES FACING NEXT PRESIDENT
- FIRST AMMENDMENT RELIGIOUS FREEDOM
- SAME SEX ILLEGAL MARRIAGE
- ABORTION HARVESTING and SELLING BODY PARTS OF

UNBORN CHILDREN
- CYBER SPACE & SOCIAL MEDIA CRIMES
- QUALITY EDUCATION • CRIME and DELINQUENCY

EMPLOYMENT and EMPLOYMENT PREPARATION.
- COMBAT HOMELESSNESS

NATIONAL and INTERNATIONAL INTEREST
- SUPPORT FOR ISRAEL

STOP TERRORIST INVASIONS

<u>First Amendment - Religion and Expression</u>: "Congress shall make no law respecting an establishment of religion, or prohibiting the free exercise thereof; or abridging the freedom of speech, or of the press; or the right of the people peaceably to assemble, and to petition the Government for a redress of grievances". The new Administration is very likely to face the religious freedom question. There may be attempts to restrict the practice and free exercise of religious expression in the market place

There is very likely to be inner conflict with "moral law" and natural law. That is God's law vs man's law. One may be put in position to choose God's law over Man's law. AN EXAMPLE OF CONFLICTING ELEMENTS

GRAYSON, Ky. — After five nights in jail for refusing to issue marriage licenses to same-sex couples, Kim Davis, a Kentucky county clerk, walked free Tuesday to a roar of cheers from thousands of supporters, but she and her lawyer would not say whether she would continue to defy court orders and try to block the licenses. Outside the jail here, a planned demonstration by people who, like Ms. Davis, say that same-sex marriage violates their religious beliefs turned buoyant when she was released, the sense of triumph mixed with a dose of presidential politics. Many legal strategist do not agree with Ms. Davis action and see it as the wrong fight to pick. However, the fight '*will not be between those well versed in natural law and the opposition but, common lay persons who are every day God fearing people who know a lot about the Bible in their Country where the Bible and Christianity is foundational. So, resistance to same sex marriage is coming from many directions. We have to hold fast to what we know is right. It doesn't take a Scientist or an Anthropologist to know the difference and purpose of male and female. If we don't stand for what we know is right, we will fall for anything. Reputable scholars and many learned men and women conclude that the Supreme Court has violated the constitution by making a law involving religion.......Marriage was designed by God and sanctioned by divine authority and revelation. We support Ms Davis to the limit. One thing she knows, same sex entanglement being called marriage is dead wrong.

THE CHURCH and SAME SEX MARRIAGE

Same Sex Marriage — This is a social ill with various contributory factors. The more sophisticated species in the animal kingdom (man and woman) are subject to emotion, perception and complicated inordinate affection. Unlike other species of the animal kingdom, humans are not programmed for limited cycles where the animal is in heat. Humans by virtue of the psyche are open to intuition, imagination, sensory perception, dreams and extraneous abnormal thoughts and desires. From this comes addiction, perversion, homosexuality and deception from the spirit world. Same sex marriage is the culmination of these inner conflicts not the cause. In general all earlier societies rejected the notion that there were no prevention or cure for these abnormalities. It is not unusual that a boy may have features like his mother or a girl may have her father's features. But if the biology and the physiology is clearly distinctive, then the identity should follow suit. The identity has a lot to do with environment and parenting. Don't associate with the chickens if you don't intend to be one. Teach the child that he/she is in charge of their identity and destiny and they can do all things through Christ.

The "CAN DO" message resonates far more than the "CAN'T" message. Through conditioning, many types of objects or situations can become sexually stimulating-particularly among preadolescents and adolescents-including erotic literature, sex scenes in plays and films, pictures of nude or partially nude individuals, and underclothing or other objects intimately associated with potential sexual' partners. . Sexual arousal may also accompany strong emotional reactions — such as fear and excitement especially if associated with the performance of some forbidden act. Consequently without defense mechanisms such as consciousness toward God and knowledge of His Word conceived in intimacy, one's mind and emotions may be carried in all directions resulting in deviant behavior. One must soundly resist and reject the onslaught of deviant behavior. Abnormal Psychology and Modern Life Carson, Butcher and Coleman, 1988.

Pedophilia - Pedophilia is not pronounced very loudly but if it raises its voice, it is snuffed out rather quickly. There is no attempt to explain its origin or normalize its practice. "CONTROL" is the word don't even think about coming out of the closet.

Variant Sexual Behavior — in-variant sexual behavior such as pedophilia and homosexuality, satisfaction is dependent primarily on something other than a mutually desired sexual engagement with sexually mature members of the opposite gender. So defined, a vast array of preference patterns are comprised in which the sexual development of the affected individual has for some reason deviated from the standard, adult heterosexual course. This deviation has a psychological base not a biological or a physiological base. Consequently it is learned, or thought, or conceived from the environment whether through explicit music, language, pornographic pictures, or accepted societal norms created by a fallen degenerate culture. When such negative stimuli is conceived, it may require supernatural power to break it before it runs it's course. The best antidote is physical removal from the scene. Disengagement will neutralize aggressive stimuli and establish normal logical reasoning.

What does the Bible say? "Then when lust hath conceived, it bringeth forth sin: and sin, when it is finished, bringeth forth death." James1:15

You must control your thinking. Don't allow all kinds of mental garbage to be deposited in your mind. Think on these things

"Finally, brothers and sisters, whatever is true, whatever is noble, whatever is right, whatever is pure, whatever is . lovely, whatever is admirable—if anything is excellent or praiseworthy--think about such things". Philippians 4:8.

CONCLUSION

Same agents found in pedophilia are found in homosexuality and other deviant behaviors. Society demands that the pedophile control his deviant sexual drives and behave according to the accepted societal norms. This may be done in many ways that are not repressive. What one believes plays a major part in controlling behavior. Conceiving the positive and displacing the negative is productive and successful. Counseling can be highly instructive in shaping the kind of mental attitude desired and finding peaceful solutions where there may be conflicts.

Isn't it interesting that the one who brought peaceful solutions to mankind is JESUS CHRIST? JESUS SAID: John 14:27

Peace I leave with you, My peace I give to you; not as the world gives do I give to you. Let not your heart be troubled, neither let it be afraid".

Peace that Jesus gives overcomes repression. Your prayer life will result in peace when coupled together with obedience to God's Word. The road to same sex marriage began with unrecognized deviant behavior. It was not treated as pedophilia is treated, was not condemned, and therefore not treated. Great conflict arises in the Church over this issue because the bible clearly openly condemns the practice of homosexuality. Neither the homosexual, nor any other person involved in deviant behavior is condemned any more than fornicators, adulterers, liars are condemned. The practice is condemned not the person. True confession and real repentance will be required by the true church in What does the Bible say? "Then when lust hath conceived, it bringeth forth sin: and sin, when it is finished, bringeth forth death." James1:15

You must control your thinking. Don't allow all kinds of mental garbage to be deposited in your mind. Think on these things

"Finally, brothers and sisters, whatever is true, whatever is noble, whatever is right, whatever is pure, whatever is . lovely, whatever is admirable—if anything is excellent or praiseworthy--think about such things". Philippians 4:8.

CONCLUSION

Same agents found in pedophilia are found in homosexuality and other deviant behaviors. Society demands that the pedophile control his deviant sexual drives and behave according to the accepted societal . norms. This may be done in many ways that are not repressive. What one believes plays a major part in controlling behavior. Conceiving the positive and displacing the negative is productive and successful.

Counseling can be highly instructive in shaping the kind of mental attitude desired and finding peaceful solutions where there may be conflicts.

Isn't it interesting that the one who brought peaceful solutions to mankind is JESUS CHRIST? JESUS SAID: John 14:27

Peace I leave with you, My peace I give to you; not as the world gives do I give to you. Let not your heart be troubled, neither let it be afraid".

Peace that Jesus gives overcomes repression. Your prayer life will result in peace when coupled together with obedience to God's Word. The road to same sex marriage began with unrecognized deviant behavior. It was not treated as pedophilia is treated, was not condemned, and therefore not treated. Great conflict arises in the Church over this issue because the bible clearly openly condemns the practice of homosexuality. Neither the homosexual, nor any other person involved in deviant behavior is condemned any more than fomicators, adulterers, liars are condemned. The practice is condemned not the person. True confession and real repentance will be required by the true church in order for true fellowship and participation in the sacraments to be administered. Churches should make sure their by-laws and job descriptions have clear language on required behavior for officers and employees and expected behavior for all members. All members are expected to persevere in the Christian walk.

Churches must state clearly up front their position on same sex marriage. The Supreme Court ruling on same sex marriage does not supersede the first amendment.

The church is open to the public for worship, for prayer and participation in any and all religious and social services provided by the church so long as participation is lawful, reasonable and for the right purpose. The church tax exempt status enables the church to offer services, provide food, education, counseling, temporary shelter, aid to families and many other community and family needs without racial, gender, orientation or natural origin discrimination. The church does not condone, promote, or permit practices of adultery, fornication, homosexuality or any acts of deviant behavior. The church invites and encourages all sinners to choose to come for cleansing whether involved in deviant life style, social deviance or personal sinful life style, the gospel of Jesus Christ has a strong reputation over thousands of years and millions of people of changing lives from the most depraved conditions.

A statement of the church regarding same sex marriage and any involvement therein by the church or any minister or leader of the church is that it is totally forbidden. The Episcopal Bishop has stated well the church position.

"As the Episcopal Bishop of the Diocese of Rhode Island, I firmly support the traditional definition of marriage as the union between one male and one female. I believe that Holy Matrimony is a sacred religious rite, whose definition should not be re-interpreted by legislation or civil courts. "A Divine Institution. The Bible presents marriage as a divine institution. If marriage were of human origin, then human beings would have a right to decide the kind of marital relationships to choose. Marriage, however, began with God. It was established by God at the beginning of human history when He "created the heavens and the earth" (Gen 1:1). As the Creator of marriage, God has the right to tell us which principles should govern our marital relationships. If God had left us no instructions about marriage after establishing it , then marriage could be regulated according to personal whims. But He has not left us in the dark. In His revelation contained in the pages of the Bible, God has revealed His will regarding the nature and function of marriage. As Christians who choose to live in accordance with God's will, we must study and respect those Biblical principles governing marriage, divorce, and remarriage. In some instances, the laws of a state regarding marriage, divorce and remarriage ignore or even violate the teachings of the Bible. In such cases, as Christians, "we must obey God rather than men" (Acts 5:29).

Samuele Bacchiocchi, Ph. D., Andrews University

Marriage is a divine institution instituted by God and is a religious institution typical of the union between Christ and the Church. We will not violate the laws of

God in order to satisfy the State or political correctness. We will not perform mock wedding ceremonies involving same sex partners.

Supreme Court is in violation of the first amendment

DEFENDERS OF CHURCH AND STATE
Chief Justice Roberts
Associate Justice Clearance Thomas
Justice Antonin Scalia
Justice Samuel Alito

THESE ARE THE BRAVE MEN WHOSE DEFENSE OF THE CONSTITUTION PRESERVES THE TRUE VALUE and QURLITY OF LIFE WHICH DISTINGUISHED AMERICA FROM OTHER NATIONS

The Supreme Court ruled 5-4 that the Constitution requires that same-sex couples be allowed to marry no matter where they live and that states may no longer reserve the right only for heterosexual couples. Supreme

Court rules gay couples nationwide have a right to marrv.

Chief Justice Roberts

He delved into the history of marriage and wrote that other cases that had changed aspects of marriage like the Loving case - but none until now had changed its core structure as being between a man and a woman.

The chief justice also suggested that the logic applied by the majority to same-sex marriage might also be employed to defend polygamy, writing, "It is striking how much of the majority's reasoning would apply with equal force to the claim of a fundamental right to plural marriage."

Associate Justice Clarence Thomas

Thomas interpreted "liberty" in the due process clause of the 14th Amendment as referring specifically to "freedom from restraint." With that in mind, he wrote that the petitioners couldn't claim "under the most plausible definition of 'liberty,' that they have been imprisoned or physically restrained by the States for participating in same-sex relationships," noting that they have "been left alone to order their lives as they see fit. "What they had not been granted by the states is the formal recognition of their marriages in a formal way, and Thomas argued, "Liberty is only freedom from governmental action, not of its offspring; it is the catalyst that produces lust, sex, and divorce. A healthy marriage depends first on moral consciousness. If we are to have life proper, abundant life, full and complete, we can only derive such a life from the Master Mind. God is omniscient, omnipresent, and omnipotent. He is holy, eternal, and immutable. In order for there to be a duplication, there has to be an original. There must be a pattern to copy, a standard to measure by, a true form, a mark of perfection, a "right way" and a "wrong way". Such a design, such an infinite order of intelligence

THESE ARE THE BRAVE MEN WHOSE DEFENSE OF THE

CONSTITUTION PRESERVES THE TRUE VALUE and QUALITY OF LIFE WHICH DISTINGUISHED AMERICA FROM OTHER NATIONS The Supreme Court ruled 5-4 that the Constitution requires that same-sex couples be allowed to marry no matter where they live and that states may no longer reserve the right only for heterosexual couples. Supreme

Court rules gay couples nationwide have a right to marrv.

Chief Justice Roberts

He delved into the history of marriage and wrote that other cases that had changed aspects of marriage like the Loving case - but none until now had changed its core structure as being between a man and a woman.

The chief justice also suggested that the logic applied by the majority to same-sex marriage might also be employed to defend polygamy, writing, "It is striking how much of the majority's reasoning would apply with equal force to the claim of a fundamental right to plural marriage."

Associate Justice Clarence Thomas

Thomas interpreted "liberty" in the due process clause of the 14th Amendment as referring specifically to "freedom from restraint." With that in mind, he wrote that the petitioners couldn't claim "under the most plausible definition of 'liberty,' that they have been imprisoned or physically restrained by the States for participating in same-sex relationships," noting that they have "been left alone to order their lives as they see fit. "What they had not been granted by the states is the formal recognition of their marriages in a formal way, and Thomas argued, "Liberty is only freedom from governmental action, not an entitlement to governmental benefits. "Thomas' criticism of the majority was scathing: "Perhaps recognizing that these case do not actually involve liberty as it has been understood, the majority goes to great lengths to assert that its decision advance the 'dignity' of same-sex couples... The flaw in that reasoning, of course, is that the Constitution contains no 'dignity' Clause, and even if it did, the government would be incapable of bestowing dignity. "

And he maintained that the court had "short- circuit[ed]" the political process by not allowing states to define marriage for themselves, and he predicted the majority's decision could have 'potentially ruinous consequences for religious liberty. "Marriage is a divine institution predetermined by God with permanent and specific construction based on original design of the genders for a specific purpose.

The purpose and / or design is fixed with immutable specific practices which cannot be crossed without being abominable, fruitless and obnoxious.

The constitution does not require that same sex couples be allowed to marry. FIVE JUSTICES REQUIRE THAT SAME SEX UNIONS BE RECOGNIZED. These are not elected men and women representing constituents and allowing the democratic process to function. Rather the democratic process is circumvented by five justices who through judicial activism have imposed their liberalism on the represented body and deprived them of the right to be represented in this matter by their representatives which is constitutional. As Justice Roberts has stated, no changes to marriages by the courts have ever sought to change its core structure from being between one man and one woman. Who God has fixed is set in stone. It is consistent with the design. The psychology and the biology follow the design when normal function is in place. Procreation requires heterosexual attraction this attraction leads to the production of offspring. Abnormal homosexual attraction is not consistent with the design and purpose for which the design exists.

Chief Justice Roberts Continued:

"The majority today relies on its own understanding of what freedom is and must become," he said to the court, and the deepest problem with their decision was "the disrespect it shows the democratic process." With this decision, proponents of same-sex marriage lost the opportunity to win acceptance through the democratic process, he said, and "they lose this just when the winds of change were freshening at their backs. "Five lawyers," he said, deemed themselves chosen, "to burst the bonds of history."

Associate Justice Antonin Scalia

Scalia mocked the majority in his dissent, calling the opinion "judicial Putsch," said that it was filled with "straining-to-be-memorable passages." He also wrote, "The opinion is couched in a style that is as pretentious as its content is egotistic.

Associate Justice Samuel Alito

Alito stood up for marriage as tradition that goes back for millennial , saying it was "inextricably linked" to procreation. He also wrote about religious liberty in his dissent, saying the decision "will be used to vilify Americans who are unwilling to assent to the new orthodoxy. "

Rev. Appolles Sweatte wrote: (Marriage Divorce and the Believer),

Vantage Press, 1988,

"A staggering number of people today are ready to undo in a matter of weeks what was intended for life. According to reports, approximately 50 percent of the marriages formed in our modern-day society end in divorce. Yes there is something grossly wrong with our society. It has eaten the bitter herbs of humanism and drank the deadly poison of atheism. It does not have God in conscious awareness and cannot provide a climate for successful marriages. A society without morals and values cannot contribute to the success of its offspring; it is the catalyst that produces lust, sex, and divorce. A healthy marriage depends first on moral consciousness.

If we are to have life proper, abundant life, full and complete, we can only derive such a life from the Master Mind. God is omniscient, omnipresent, and omnipotent. He is holy, eternal, and immutable. In order for there to be a duplication, there has to be an original. There must be a pattern to copy, a standard to measure by, a true form, a mark of perfection, a "right way" and a "wrong way". Such a design, such an high order of intelligence can only be found in God and those to whom His Word is revealed. "Man shall not live by bread alone but by the Word of God (Luke 4:4). Marriage is a divine institution, constituted at the beginning before the origin of human society The Creator made man male and female, and ordained marriage as the indispensable condition of the continuance of the race (Gen. 1:27-28). He implanted social affections and desires in man's nature. He made marriage an ennobling influence powerfully contributing to the development of a complete life in man and woman. The support systems for a free society keeping it morally sound and socially just, are "God, "the family" and the "home". It is when man loses his identity with God that he becomes carnal, sensual, and devilish. The marriage suffers and the home is broken"

BUZZ WORDS and BUSINESS

Politics has coined certain buzz words which they elasticize and move in any direction so as to create a form that may be completely the opposite of the original. Such terms as "rights require gay" or certain phrase as "right to choose" while the mother has the right to choose, she takes away the baby's right to life. In the Supreme Court's majority opinion, the constitution requires that same sex couples be allowed to marry. And that gay couples nationwide have the right to marry. John F. Kennedy Proclaiming that rights, come not from the State, but from the hand of Almighty God.

Marriage is already defined by God. This, that the Supreme Court is authorizing is not marriage it's fake, phony, rejected by God, immoral, contributes nothing to society, introduces a foul image and a corrupt relationship which will damage children that may be involved. To say that the constitution REQUIRES this abomination shows the effect of gross elasticization. Of course these are justices the constitution says whatever they want it to say. As President John F. Kennedy said: "Rights come not from the State, but from the hand of the Almighty God". God has not given anyone the right to re-define marriage.

THE CLAIM TO RIGHTS

The claim to "rights" finds itself in many places and with •many faces. Since the successful demand for Civil Rights in the 1960's, where basic human rights were denied African Americans solely based on natural origin, on their physical being at birth without choice or right to choose regarding their physical being, every undeserving group want to claim that their deviant behavior deserves to be called a Civil Rights issue. African Americans Because they were born black were easily identified and targeted for abuse. They were stereotyped and abused. They had no closet to go in, no place to hide. They were rejected in the public square as someone with leprosy. They were pushed to the back and denied due process. Their physical lives were . made a living hell. Yet they wanted to fight in the white folks army and defend the freedom they were surely to be denied. They had to fight like hell for privileges others had simply by virtue of being born Now, someone comes along, develops a deviant behavior, such as an abnormal attraction, becomes an alcoholic or drug addict, or maybe a pedophile. These practices are to be included under the umbrella of Civil Rights??? There are no rights based on the way one chooses to have sex. There are no "gay rights" the so-called gay community is protected under the 14th amendment like everybody else. Being gay, or being homosexual, or being a pedophile is not a right it's a temporary fallen state that one can overcome. There are many behavioral deficiencies some children have to overcome. The behavior is rejected and the child grows and breaks free because deviant behavior is displaced and correct behavior is assimilated.

People of faith should not accept deviant behavior exemplified by their children. This society is out off center with the moral code. Those with God . consciousness ask the question, "what did God say?" When they know that, that becomes ground zero. Confer with your pediatrician to clear any medical conditions. If you accept the Word of God as absolute authority, you have the basis that empower you to speak with authority. The child needs your help not your pity or sympathy, Mark 1 1:22-23 "Jesus answering said unto them: "HAVE FAITH IN GOD". For verily I say unto you, that whosoever shall SAY unto this mountain "BE THOU REMOVED" and shall not doubt in his heart but shall believe that those things "WHICH HE IS SAYING" shall come to pass, he shall have whatsoever he says.

1. When you pray believe that you receive and you shall have .

2. When you stand praying forgive if you have ought against any that your heavenly Father may forgive you your trespasses.

YOUR STATE OF MIND HAS A LOT TO DO WITH EVERYTHING. Your level of God consciousness is reflected in your temperament, tone of voice, seriousness of your statements, your facial expression says whether or not you believe what you are saying.

Because the Supreme Court Justices are not in line with God, they have grossly misled the public. Their decision puts a nail in America's coffin, further corrupts America's youth, teaches youths to be irresponsible, not to resist temptation, not to fight against negativity, not to be resilient and not to overcome obstacles. Our country falls way behind in education.

According to Pearson, the United States has a "cognitive skills and educational attainment" score of 0.39, which makes the United States <u>rank fourteenth</u> out of forty countries ranked in that category. The top ten countries (and their scores) are:

1. South Korea (1.30)
2. Japan (1.03)
3. Singapore (0.99)
4. Hong Kong (0.96)
5. Finland (0.92)
6. United Kingdom (0.67)
7. Canada (0.60) .
8. Netherlands (0.58)
9. Ireland (0.51)

Cognitive skills predict academic performance, so schools that improve academic performance might also improve cognitive skills. To investigate the impact schools have on both academic performance and cognitive skills, we related standardized achievement-test scores to measures of cognitive skills in a large sample ($N = 1,367$) of eighth-grade students attending traditional, exam, and charter public schools. Test scores and gains in test scores over time correlated with measures of cognitive skills

A. Cognitive skills predict academic performance

B. Schools that improve academic performance also improve cognitive skills

C. Growing importance of cognitive skills in wage determination

D. Faith plays an integral part in cognitive development. (a Biblical values)

The school system suffers for lack of definite policies that provoke training, self-discipline, and respect for leadership. OR, it fails to enforce its policies which are designed to bring positive results. Without the cooperation and participation of the parents school cannot fill the role of parents, do social work and be educators at the same time. It is really the parents place to make sure the child arrives at school prepared and ready to learn. Leadership that encourages youth . to conform to proven standards and acquire a winner's mentality winning the victory over personal insurmountable obstacles is the kind of leadership we need from the Supreme Court. Same sex dilemma has been around throughout the centuries. No society in the history of the world has agreed to glamorize its practice or honor its deviant behavior. Supreme Court has sent a message that if you complain enough, cry enough, demonstrate enough, you can change the law. Perhaps the pedophile will be next he will expect the court to legalize his practice.

WISDOM DOES NOT COME HORIZONTALLY

WISDOM COMES VERTICALLY We rely on the Supreme Court to act with wisdom, good judgment, sound reasoning, and to fulfill that which is the specific purpose assigned to the position they hold. Since the" 5 Justices have ruled against God, against morals, and against values revealed by divine revelation from the beginning of time, those following their lead can only decline and go down. They offer rights they cannot give. They seek to force the constitution to require that which has never been required and which the founding fathers would totally disdain. They would do well to consult the Bible as the founding fathers did and produced wise decisions. Mental preparation and the power to make right choices are virtues that distinguish leaders from failures. The ability to face challenges and overcome obstacles even those that appear to be inherited or may even be inherited, however, are subject to the power of the mind. Wise men, men of faith and God consciousness do not assign those who have fallen, to the pit, but rather realize that by setting standards that are more in line with the nature of God provide the impetus that shape positive thinking and ultimately result in new more acceptable behavior. WE CAN LIVE BY THE WORD OF GOD AND BE HAPPY. Those abnormalities or deficiencies or handicaps in life which are not in line with the original design, though they be beyond the reach of human hands, they are subject to the power within you when you believe. The level of FAITH in the Country depends on the quality of men and women holding office. When the Government demonstrates faith in God it signals a certain belief and life style that is emulated in the public square and in the public school. Life in America as we know it today with out of-control behavior, disregard for life, attack on schools, churches, and other public entities, demonstrates how far we are from God.

George Washington and FAITH By 1778, George Washington had so often witnessed God's intervention that on August 20, he wrote Thomas Nelson that: "The Hand of providence has been so conspicuous in all this, that he must be worse than an infidel that lacks faith, and more than wicked, that has not gratitude enough to acknowledge his obligations".

DANGERS OF A REPROBATE MIND

All of these deviances from normal behavior are MIND diseases. Minds are plastic and can be shaped early in life to fit the accepted norm. It is ludicrous to think that God would create a perfectly normal physical male body, then give it the mind of a female to go along with the male genitalia. No, the deviation is in the mind. As a man thinks in his heart so is he: Proverbs 23:7. Train a child according to his/her inclination and when he/she is old, they won't forget it. The assimilations of sound truth will override negative false desires.

Our view of ourselves as male or female, the social demands made upon us for playing our expected sexual role, our concept of what sexual behavior is appropriate, and our anticipation of what will be exciting and pleasurable—all these are for the most part learned, and they help determine the sexual practices we develop as adults. And through conditioning, many types of objects or situations can become -sexually stimulating-particularly among preadolescents and adolescents-including erotic literature, sex scenes in plays and films, pictures of nude or partially nude individuals, and underclothing or other objects intimately associated with potential sexual partners. Sexual1 arousal may also accompany strong emotional reactions-such as fear and excitement especially if associated with the performance of some forbidden act. Given the many channels that human sexual interest may take, especially when for some reason the usual patterning has become blocked, it is hardly surprising that many persons find their principal sexual satisfactions in practices outside the range of what is considered acceptable or normal in the given culture. The sexual drive is normally sufficiently powerful to override all but the most severe social sanctions; thus we see variant sexual needs frequently erupting into variant sexual behavior. Variant sexual behavior is behavior in which satisfaction is dependent primarily on something other than a mutually desired sexual engagement with a sexually mature member of the opposite gender. So defined, the domain encompasses a vast array of preference patterns in which the sexual development of the affected individual has for some reason deviated from the standard, adult heterosexual course. As already observed, the specter of these sexual variants seems peculiarly threatening to many people in our society, and expressions of tolerance for such behavior as homosexuality, for example, can arouse intense emotion. It is certainly true that some forms of sexual variation, such as rape and child molestation, are contrary to the welfare of society and its members. Other forms, however, are generally victimless and thus constitute no obvious, rationally based threat to the public order. For this reason, we make a distinction between *victimless* sexual variants-in which the acts involved do not infringe on the rights of noninvolved others and/or are engaged in by mutually consenting adults and are nonharmful to the partners-and sexual deviations that involve non-consent or assault. In the former category, we would place gender identity disorders, uncomplicated male and female, homosexuality, most cases of fetishism and transvestism. The more problematic of the sexual variants, from the standpoint of the welfare of society, include voyeurism, exhibitionism, sexual sadism and masochism, pedophilia, incest, and rape. In most jurisdictions,, laws against acts in the latter category not only exist but are actively enforced. It is important to note that we have chosen *not* to follow the lead of DSM-III-R in respect to the categories of variant behavior. (Abnormal Psychology and Modern life. 1988). Robert C. Carson, James N. Butcher, James C. Coleman. It is the call of God and His Church, His Apostles and Prophets to have knowledge in this area where dynamic escapes the physical realm and enjoys information through revelation. We have to talk about demonology, spiritual gifts and divine revelation. The person whom is the only authority in this field is Jesus Christ. Moms and Dads bring your children to Jesus don't take them to the butcher. There is nothing too hard for God. Your Godly teaching to your children early in life (from birth), will be an authoritative defense. "THUS SAITH THE LORD" is a command that makes demons flee, makes the crooked straight and frees your children's mind from perversion NOTHING is hard for the LORD.

GOD IS OUR SOURCE FOR KNOWLEDGE AND VICTTORY.

1. Since the creation of the world God's invisible attributes are clearly seen, Being understood by the things that are made even His Eternal Power and Godhead so that you are without excuse because although they knew God by virtue of creation, they did not glorify Him as God nor was thankful but became futile in their THOUGHTS and their foolish hearts were darkened**. They failed to teach their children the fear of the Lord which would direct their focus on true love**.

2. They became fools changing the image of God into beastly passions therefore God gave them up to vile passions. Even their women exchanged the natural use for what is against nature (sexual deviance). Likewise the men leaving the natural use of the woman burned in their lust for one another, men with men committing what is SHAMEFUL and receiving in themselves the penalty of their error. **They didn't like to retain God in their knowledge, God gave them over to a debased mind to do those things which are not fitting being filled with all unrighteousness, sexual immorality, wickedness, covetousness, maliciousness; full of envy murder, strife deceit, evil mindedness, inventors of evil things, disobedient to parents. (Romans Chapter 1).**

3. **In order to have a sound mind, one must have knowledge of the TRUTH. That knowledge comes with the knowledge of whom God is. (Mark 8:27).**

POWER OF POSITIVE RELATIONSHIP

James Adams Without religion, this world would be something not fit to be mentioned in polite company: I mean hell. The Christian religion is, above all the religions that ever prevailed or existed in ancient or modern times, the religion of wisdom, virtue, equity and humanity.

The only "religion" contributing bountifully and extemporaneously, as though inspired to the progress and success of the United States is Christianity. HERE 6/11/22

The State is Never to be Separated From the Church

I exhort therefore, that, first of all, supplications, prayers, intercessions, and giving of thanks, be made for all men; For kings, and for all that are in authority; that we may lead a quiet and peaceable life in all godliness and honesty. For this is good and acceptable in the sight of God our Saviour; Who will have all men to be saved, and to come unto the knowledge of the truth. (1 Timothy 2: 1-4).

> The State enjoys an advisory relationship with the Church. The true Church is exemplary and strategic in demonstrating intrinsic core values that characterize qualities that are always at the base of success.

> The State will die when it chooses to disconnect and disassociate with the institution of life, the source of wisdom. The church makes no laws but is rather subject to the Constitution of the United States. However the church recognizes a moral obligation to proclaim that the laws of nature are subject to the laws of nature's God. The Country is greatly benefited when intangible values and qualities characterize its representatives. The Church will never die for the gates of hell shall not prevail. It is written: "on this rock I will build my church, and the gates of hell cm shall not prevail against it". (Matthew 16:17)

Dynamics of learned behavior

Compilation of Social Security act comprising 8 standards.

By Dr. Appolles Sweatte Psychologist

THE HOI POLLOI

Many young people engage in sexual risk behaviors that can result in unintended health outcomes for" example among U.S. high school students surveyed in 2013,

47% had ever had sexual intercourse

34% had had sexual intercourse during the previous 3 months and of these,

CONGRESSIONAL STANDS FOR ABSTINENCE SEPARAT£ PROGRAM FOR ABSTINENCE EDUCATION SEX EDUCATION PROGRAM UNDER SEC. 510. [42 U.S.C. 710] (a)

A. Has as its specific purpose, teaching the social psychological and health gains to be realized by abstaining from sexual activity.

B. Teaches abstinence from sexual activity outside of marriage as the expected standard for all school age children

C. Teaches that abstinence from sexual activity is the only certain way to avoid out-of-wedlock pregnancy, sexual transmitted diseases and other associated health problems.

Teaches that a mutually faithful monogamous relationship in context of marriage is the expected standard of human sexual activity.

Teaches that sexual activity outside of the context of marriage is likely to have harmful psychological and physical effects

Teaches that bearing out-of-wedlock is likely to have harmful consequences for he child, the child's parents and society.

Teaches young people how to reject sexual advances and how alcohol and drug use increases vulnerability to sexual advances; and

Teaches the importance of attaining self-sufficiency before engaging in sexual activity.

BIBLICAL DEFINITION

Question: "What does the Bible say about the form of church government?" Answer: The Lord was very clear in His Word about how He wishes His church on earth to be organized and managed. First, Christ is the head of the church and its supreme authority (Ephesians 1 :22; 4: 15; Colossians 1: 18). Second, the local church is to be autonomous, free from any external authority or control, with the right of self-government and freedom from the interference of any hierarchy of individuals or organizations (Titus 1 :5). Third, the church is to be governed by spiritual leadership consisting of two main offices-elders and deacons." Elders" were a leading body among the Israelites since the time of Moses. We find them making political decisions (2 Samuel 5:3; 2 Samuel) 17:4, 15), advising the king in later history (1 Kings 20:7), and representing the people concerning spiritual matters (Exodus 7: 17; 24:1, Numbers 11:16, 24-25). The early Greek translation of the Old Testament, the Septuagint, used the Greek word *presbuteros* for "elder." This is the same Greek word used in the New Testament that is also translated "elder." The New Testament refers a number of times to elders who served in the role of church leadership (Acts 14:23, 15:2, 20:17; Titus 1 :5; James 5:14) and apparently each church had more than one, as the word is usually found in the plural. The only exceptions refer to cases in which one elders being singled out for some reason (1 Timothy 5:1, 19). In the Jerusalem church, elders were part of the leadership along with the apostles (Acts 15:2-16:4). It seems that the position of elder was equal to the position f episkopos, translated "overseer" or "bishop" (<u>Acts 1 1 :30</u>; 1.11m.Q.tbL5LIZ). The

. term elder may refer to the dignity of the office, while the term bishop/overseer describes its authority and duties (<u>1 Peter 2:25</u>, <u>5:1-4</u>). . In <u>Philippians 1 : 1</u>, Paul greets the bishops and deacons but does not mention the elders, presumably because the elders are the same as the bishops. Likewise, <u>1 Timothy 3:21</u> @ gives the qualifications of bishops and deacons but not of elders. <u>Titus 1:5-7</u> seems also to tie these two terms together. The position of "deacon," from diakonos, meaning "through the dirt," was one of servant leadership to the church. Deacons are separate from elders, while having qualifications that are in many ways similar to those of elders (<u>1 Timothy 3:8-13</u>). Deacons assist the church in whatever is needed, as recorded in Acts chapter 6. Concerning the word poimen, translated "pastor" in reference to a human leader of a church, it is found only once in the New Testament, in <u>Ephesians 4:11</u>: "It was he who gave some to be apostles, some to be prophets, some to be evangelists, and some to be pastors and teachers." Most associate the two terms "pastors" and "teachers" as referring to a single position, a pastor-teacher. It is likely that a pastor teacher was the spiritual shepherd of a particular local church. It would seem from the above passages that there was always a plurality of elders, but this does not negate God's gifting particular elders with the teaching gifts while gifting others with the gift of administration, prayer, etc. (<u>Romans 12:3g</u>; <u>Ephesians 4:11</u>).

Nor does it negate God's calling them into a ministry in which they will use those gifts (<u>Acts 13:1</u>). Thus, one elder may emerge as the "pastor," another may do the majority of visiting members because he has the gift of compassion, while another may "rule" in the sense of handling organizational details. Many churches that are organized with a pastor and deacon board perform the functions of a plurality of elders in that they share the ministry load and work together in some decision making. In Scripture there was also much congregational input into decisions. Thus, a "dictator" leader who makes the decisions (whether called elder, or bishop, or pastor) is unscriptural (Acts 1 :23, 26; 6:3, §; 15:22, 30; 2 Corinthians 8: 19). So, too, is a congregation-ruled church that does not give weight to the elders' or church leaders' input. In summary, the Bible teaches a leadership consisting of a plurality of elders (bishops/overseers) along with a group of deacons who serve the church. But it is not contrary to this plurality of elders to have one of the elders serving in the major "pastoral" role. God calls some as "pastor/teachers" (even as He called some to be missionaries in Acts 13)and gives them as gifts to the church (Ephesians 4:11). Thus, a church may have many elders, but not all elders are called to serve in the pastoral role. But, as one of the elders, the pastor or "teaching elder has no more authority in decision making than does any other elder.

CHURCH CONSTITUTION, SEXUALITY, and GENDER

For the most part, a church's articles of faith will lay out the basic beliefs of the church regarding the Bible, God, Christ, man, sin, salvation, the church, ordinances and office, membership and perhaps a handful of other things. This raises the question of marriage, sexuality, and gender identity-where do they fit in a statement of belief? Do they even belong in the first place? Within a classical understanding of doctrine, a statement regarding marriage, sexuality, and gender identity could fit easily under the category of anthropology. The doctrine of anthropology is the study of human nature and existence. This doctrine asks the questions: Who am I? How did I get here? What is my purpose in life?

The best place to start in answering those questions is the first chapters of Genesis. Here we see some key truths about human nature that we must not forget. First, we are created by God—that is how we got here (Gen 1:26—27). Next, we are created in God's image (Gen 1:26—27). While the image of God includes a number of different aspects, we can at least affirm that it includes the fact that we are created for a relationship with God. Third, we have been given stewardship over the rest of creation (Gen 1:26, 28), which means that we have the unique responsibility of caring for everything else God has made. Fourth, we see that God created us in two distinct genders—male and female (Gen 1.'27). And finally, we recognize that God intended for the man and woman to "be fruitful and multiply, and fill the earth" (Gen 1:28). These points will become very important as we see below.

When we move to Genesis 2, we learn about how mankind is created to relate to one another. In verse 18 we read, "Then the Lord God said, 'It is not good for the man to be alone; I will make him a helper suitable for him.'" In the verses that follow, we see the creation of the woman and the first marriage.

God takes one of Adam's ribs and fashions the woman out of it (Gen '2:21— 22). He then brings the woman to Adam and presents her to him as his "suitable partner," or his wife. In verse 23, we read Adam's response to God granting recognition that this woman is "bone of my bones, and flesh of my flesh." Finally, verse 24 gives us the divinely inspired commentary on this union. We read, "For this reason a man shall leave his father and his mother, and be joined to his wife; and they shall become one flesh." What we learn from the creation narrative is that marriage is a comprehensive union of a man and a woman in an exclusive, monogamous, covenant relationship designed to endure for a lifetime and directed toward the rearing of the next generation. Not only do the opening chapters of Genesis point out God's design for marriage, but they also lay the foundation for our understanding of gender and sexual identity. Note that God created two genders— male and female. He did not create the multiplicity of genders or sexual identities in the ever-expanding LGBTQ nomenclature. There are simply male and female, and they are designed to be complementary partners to one another. This is most clearly expressed through the institution of marriage Marriage between a man and a woman then becomes the only biblically authorized context for sexual expression. Any sexual expression apart from an exclusive, monogamous marriage between one man and one woman is sinful according to the text of Scripture. It is this understanding that we want to put into the governing documents of our churches. Thankfully, we do not need to re-create the wheel in order to get an effective statement on anthropology, marriage, and sexuality into our church constitutions and by-laws. The first place that you ought to look is the statement of faith of your own denomination. Many denominations have such statements that will give you a starting point for appropriate language to use. The statement of your denomination might not be comprehensive enough for what we face today, but it should a good place to start. You can add to those denominational resources the helpful input of groups like Alliance Defending Freedom who have composed language that could be adopted into your constitution. Their work is more generic in order to appeal across denominational lines. My preference is to combine both such resources to develop a unique statement that addresses the needs of your specific church and the distinctive of your faith tradition. For example, below is my proposed statement that I believe works well within a Southern Baptist context. **UP DATED CONSTITUTION and BY-LAWS** We believe that marriage is the uniting of one man and one woman in an exclusive, monogamous, covenant commitment for a lifetime. It is God's unique gift to reveal the union between Christ and his church and to provide for the man and the woman in marriage the framework for intimate companionship, the channel of sexual expression according to biblical standards, and the means for procreation of THE HUMSN RACE. (Gen 1:26—28; 2:18— 24; Prov 14:1; 17.•6; 18:22; Eccl 9:9; Matt 19:3—9; Mark 10:6-12; 1 Cor 5:14; 1 Pet 3:17) We believe that any form of sexual immorality (including adultery, fornication, homosexuality are all condemned. These are mind diseases it has been proven by those who have overcome by faith and therapy.

We believe that God offers redemption and restoration to all who confess and forsake their sin, seeking His mercy and forgiveness through Jesus Christ. (John 14:6; Rom 3:23; 6:23; 1 Cor 6:11; 1 John 1:9) We believe that every person must be afforded compassion, love, kindness, respect, and dignity. Hateful and harassing behavior or attitudes directed toward any individual are to be repudiated and are not in accord with scripture nor the doctrines of the church. However, identifying particular behaviors and identities as sin does not constitute harassment or hate. (1 Cor Gal 6:1; Eph 4:15, 32; James 1: 19) As churches grow and develop through the years, so do their needs. It is important to modify and update your church bylaws to address both changes to your church and changes in society. Some of these changes are straightforwrd and simple. If your church has moved locations or changed its name, it is time to amend your bylaws. Many churches have grown, and growth leads to change. For example, when your church was founded, it may not have seemed necessary to require new members to complete a new member orientation when joining the church or your church may not have had the pastoral staff to lead such an orientation. As your church has grown so has the importance of new member orientations. It is time to update your bylaws. In Obergefell v. Hodges, the United States Supreme Court legalized same-sex marriage in all 50 states. Because the church's definition of marriage may differ from the national definition, it is important for churches to proactively define marriage in their bylaws. Bylaw language defining marriage, in the biblical sense, doesn't mean that the church is immune from a lawsuit or complaint, but it reduces the likelihood of a lawsuit or complaint and places the church in a much better legal situation should a lawsuit be filed against it. If your church hasn't updated its bylaws in several years, it is time to include a biblical definition of marriage and human sexuality in your bylaws what are the essential elements we need to have in our Constitution and Bylaws

1. Name and address
2. Nonprofit status
3. Statement of purpose
4. Statement of religious beliefs
5. Membership policy
6. Church officers basics
7. Church staff basics
8. Finances
9. Dissolution clause
10. Amendment
11. Other

What should our bylaws say about church membership?

The Free Exercise Clause of the United States Constitution recognizes that churches are entitled to religious liberty and should be allowed to operate without secular interference, control, or manipulation. To ensure that the church is exercising its religious freedom, it is important that the church bylaws state a clear path to church membership. These membership provisions need to include membership eligibility, the process for acceptance as a church member, and the rights and duties of church membership. These provisions should also include the process for removing, revoking, or terminating church membership. Include how to reinstate inactive or former members and the method by which Statement of * Religious Beliefs, By including this provision, the church can ensure that a governing body is in place to issue a definitive interpretation of scripture for the church. This will provide guidance if the church ever faces a crisis situation Church bylaws should include provisions that address how offerings are counted and secured until the funds are removed from the building. The bylaws should also address record keeping, receipts, and reports. We also recommend including a method in your bylaws for forming a finance committee to be overseen by church leadership.

Well drafted bylaws provide clarification and direction in times of crisis. If the church is dealing with the removal of a minister or a termination of church membership, for example, the bylaw provisions on these matters provide the steps to be taken. Of course, the bylaws cannot anticipate every instance that may cause church conflict. This is why it is critical to identify a governing body, within the bylaws, as the authoritative interpreter of scripture for the church. If your church is in a crisis situation and you are not sure if your church bylaws provide direction on how to proceed, do not hesitate to give us a call.

POLITICAL ARENA

DEMOCRATIC PARTY

The Democratic Party as our country once knew it no longer exists. Franklin Delano Roosevelt saying a 12 . minute long prayer on national radio after announcing the bombing of Pearl Harbor; Harry S. Truman ending WWII with atomic weapons, John J. Kennedy proclaiming that rights, come from the State, but from the hand of Almighty God.

Unfortunately the very destructive elements that are at work destroying the fabric of this country come from the Democratic policy. By and large black people have blindly voted democrat not knowing whether or not it was in their best interest or in line with their core beliefs. Many social ills that brought suffering to black people were entrenched in the Democratic Party. Democrats continue to fight for corrupt and destructive policies that are destined for destruction. supreme court is used to by-pass and circumvent the will of the people as in Roe v Wade to legalize abortion on demand. The devil is dressed as an angel of light called: "woman's right to choose". The choice is fixed. The baby dies and is chopped up and sold for parts.

Democrats are happy with that and come out strong in support of "plan parenthood". History records the attitude and convictions of previous presidents who were very vocal regarding their faith. I don't know of any president who went about to make legally right that which is declared morally wrong. Most presidents if not all had great respect for the Bible and consulted it for guidance inspiration and encouragement in righteousness. In the end , the country which honored biblical doctrine and teaching , became the greatest nation on earth.

The Obama Administration has spoken and demonstrated its disregard and dissdain for American tradition and Christian values.

 This administration has done more to destroy morals and values and set the worse example for young people than Bill Clinton. This administration threw away the bible, the qur'an and everything decent and dignified, brought shame and disgrace to the nation. The entire Democratic Party should be judged by you at the polls before we are all judged by God. Remember 9/11? The country brought in unbelievers and taught them to fly our planes to our own destruction. THE NATION THAT FORGETS GOD WILL NOT SURVIVE.

"The wicked shall be turned into hell and all the nations that forget God (Psalms 9:17)

1. We have always supported Israel:

"I will bless them that bless you and curse him that curse you: and in you shall all families of the earth be blessed (Genesis 12:3). This administration has turned against Israel and has become adversarial rather than supportive.

THE REPUBLICAN PARTY HAS NOT FOUGHT AGAINST CHRISTIAN VALUES BUT NEITHER HAVE THEY SUPPORTED THEM WHOLE-HEARTEDLY

The Republican Party, also commonly called the GOP (for "Grand Old Party"), is the second oldest existing political party in the United States after its great rival, the Democratic Party. It emerged in 1854 to combat the Kansas—Nebraska Act, which threatened to extend slavery into the territories, and to promote more vigorous modernization of the economy. The Party had almost no presence in the South, but by 1858 in the North it had enlisted former <u>Whigs</u> and former <u>FreeSoil</u> Democrats to form majorities in nearly every Northern state. With its election of <u>Abraham Lincoln</u> in 1860, and its success in guiding the <u>Union</u> to victory and abolishing slavery, the party came to dominate the national political scene until 1932. The Republican Party was based on northern white Protestants, businessmen, small business owners, professionals, factory workers, farmers, and African-Americans. It was pro-business, supporting banks, the gold standard, railroads, and high tariffs to protect factory workers and grow industry faster.

Under William McKinle~ and Theodore Roosevelt, it emphasized an expansive foreign policY~. The GOP lost its majorities during the Great

Depression (1929-40). Instead, the Democrats under Franklin D. Roosevelt formed a winning "New Deal" coalition, which was dominant from 1932 through 1964. That coalition collapsed in the mid-1960s, partly because of white Southern Democrats' disaffection with passage of the Civil Rights Act of 1964. Republicans resurged, winning five of the six presidential elections 1968 to 1988, with Ronald Reagan as the party's iconic conservative hero. In recent times though, from 1992 to 2012, the Republican candidate has been elected to the White House in only two of the six presidential elections-and only in one out of those six elections, in 2004, did he win the popular vote.

Summary of historical events

(1) GOP emerged in 1854 to combat the Kansas-Nebraska Act. Which threatened to extend slavery into the territories and promote more vigorous modernization

(2) The Party had no presence in the South but by 1858 it had enlisted former Whigs and former Free Soil

Democrats to form majorities in nearly every northern state.

(3) With the election of Abraham Lincoln in 1860 the Union was guided to victory abolishing slavery and Dominated the national political scene until 1932. The Republican Party was based on northern white Protestants, businessmen, small business owners, professionals, factory workers, farmers, and African-

● Americans. It was pro-business. Could it be that the convictions of the white Protestants were influential in the fight against slavery? The voice of morality and justice had to come from somewhere. Dr. Martin Luther King Jr. was able to draw from the bank of justice because moral convictions were deposited. ● People of conscience were more likely to respond to the call of justice and set the record straight. We find ourselves again entangled in a moral dilemma. The Party doesn't matter nearly as much as the person. Men and women of quality and integrity with moral convictions can put things right. PEOPLE PERISH FOR LACK OF KNOWLEDGE

<u>Marching will never take the place of learning</u>

High School Graduation and Dropout Rates

Nationwide, 7,000 students drop out of school every day, and only about 70 percent of students graduate from high school with a high **school diploma**.

Two thousand high schools in the IJnited States produce more than half of all dropouts, and a recent study suggests that in the 50 largest cities, only 53 percent of students graduate on time. Research shows that children of color was lower for whites compared with African Americans and Latinos. The rate for Asian/Pacific Islanders was also lower than rates for Latinos and African Americans between 1989 and 2007.6 **STUDENTS MUST BE TEACHABLE**:

A country steeped in immorality without safe guards for dignity, decency, language, personality virtues and values will produce a reckless disregard for life. There will be no education without discipline, self respect and self control. These values come from home.

If the government fail to recognize a moral code, and define free speech with gutter mentality, as acceptable for the public square then disrespect will be the order of the day. If you put people in office who do not share the vision, faith or spirit of the founding fathers, you have yourself to blame for the chaos and destructive life style as we see with numerous youths and adults today. IT'S TIME FOR PEOPLE OF FAITH TO STAND UP AND TAKE BACK WHAT GOD GAVE TO THIS LAND OF THE FREE VIA THE GOSPEL OF JESUS CHRIST. JOIN FORCES WITH THE CATHOLIC CHURCH AND TEAR DOWN THE WALLS OF IMMORALITY AND GROSS UNGODLINESS, MURDER OF THE UNBORN CHILDREN, SAME SEX NARRUAGE ANDD ALL OTHER VENOMOUS DISCHARGES FROM SATANIC FORCES AND IDEOLOGY ALL WE NEED IS "WE THE PEOPLE and THE WORD OF GOD. BY ALL MEANS VOTE: BUT KNOW WHO YOU ARE VOTING FOR. DON'T LOOK AT THE PARTY LOOK AT THE PERSON SEE HOW HE / SHE VOTES ON ISSUES IMPORTANT TO YOU: FREEDOM OF RELIGION : RIGHT TO LIFE FOR THE UNBORN, FREE DECENT SPEECH NOT INDECENT SPEECH AND GUTTER LANGUAGE, RESPECT FOR SINCERELY

HELDRELIGIOUS BELIEFS PROTECTED UNDER THE 1 ST AMMENDMENT. WHEN WE GET THE COUNTRY RE-ALIGNED WITH GOD IN THE CENTER, AND WE CONTINUE TO SUPPORT ISRAEL, EVERYTHING ELSE WILL REALIZE EASY POSITIVE ADJUSTMENTS. .   GOD AND FAMILY AND COUNTRY. THIS IS THE MODEL PRIORITY ORDER FOR A SUCCESSFUL NATION.

PHILOSOPHY OF THE DEMOCRATIC PARTY According to Democrats.org, the Democratic Party believes that it is the government's responsibility to make sure businesses and other institutions serve the interest of the people. Often, Democrats paint corporations in the light of robber barons trying to take advantage of the working class. As a result, the Democratic platform normally calls for high corporate taxes, minimum wage hikes and support for unions. The belief in government's supremacy over other areas of society stems largely from progressives such as President Woodrow Wilson, who favored central planning. Franklin Roosevelt's

New Deal policies of unprecedented government involvement in the economy laid the foundation for the modern Democratic Party's support for the welfare state. In the sphere of social issues, the Democratic Party advocates an individualism according to which people are entitled to lead a chosen lifestyle without regard for traditional social norms. Members of the party typically favor expanding the definition of marriage, loosening restrictions on recreational drug use and increasing access to abortion. This philosophy is referred to as BIG GOVERNMENT, HIGH TAXES AND SOCIAL PROGRAMS. The Democratic Party thinks it's the government's responsibility to make sure business and other institutions serve the interest of the people. Re-distribution of wealth may have good intentions but fails to reach the intended goal. Receiving gifts is never as powerful and rewarding as the position of giving. When one generates capital by his or her own intuition they set the limit rather than being limited The cost of redistribution ends up making the poor poorer and the rich richer. IT IS NOT THE GOVERNMENT'S JOB TO MAKE SURE BUSINESS SERVE OTHER PEOPLE. Government would do far better if it intends to empower the people and promote individual responsibility, it should be mandatory that every male learns a trade in elementary school this may include females as well; males because it's a man's job to be the head of the house it is fixed by design. TEACH HIM TO FISH AND HE WILL EAT EVERY DAY WITHOUT THE GOVERNMENT. GIVE HIM A FISH AND HE WON'T EVEN KNOW WHERE IT CAME FROM OR HOW IT GOT THERE. Self reliance, self actualization and preparation leads to independence.

GENERAL VIEW OF THE REPUBLICAN PARTY

Differences in Philosophy   .   While there may be several differences in opinion between individual <u>Democrats</u> and <u>Republicans</u> on certain issues, what follows is a generalization of their stand on several of these issues. A Democrat is typically known as a supporter of a broader range of social services in America <u>than</u> those advocated by Republicans. Republican philosophy is based on a limited influence of government and a dominant foreign policy. Republicans are considered on the "right" end of the political spectrum while Democrats are on the "left." The far right generally is pro-re<u>ligion</u>, anti-bureaucracy, pro-military, probusiness and pro-personal responsibility. Republicans are usually considered conservative (fiscally as well as socially), may be little pious, pro-business and against the bureaucracy often associated with big government. They see big government as wasteful and an obstacle to getting things done. Their approach is Darwinian in that the strong shall survive, cream rises to the top, etc. The idea of keeping taxes low and attracting entrepreneurs; giving them a chance to get established works for everybody. Jobs come from new business not the government. THIS IS NOT JUST FOR THE SECULAR WORLD IT'S FOR ALL OF US. WE ALL PAY TAXES. WE ARE THE PEOPLE. LET'S NOT VOTE FOR THE PARTY BUT FOR THE PERSON BECAUSE HE OR SHE MEETS THE QUALIFICATIONS THAT QUALIFY THEM TO SERVE JUSTLY AND HONORABLY.

SOCIAL ISSUES FACING NEXT PRESIDENT

- FIRST AMMENDMENT RELIGIOUS FREEDOM
- SAME SEX ILLEGAL MARRIAGE

- ABORTION HARVESTING and SELLING BODY PARTS OF

UNBORN CHILDREN

- CYBER SPACE & SOCIAL MEDIA CRIMES
- QUALITY EDUCATION
- CRIME and DELINQUENCY
- EMPLOYMENT and EMPLOYMENT PREPARATION.

- COMBAT HOMELESSNESS

NATIONAL and INTERNATIONAL INTEREST

- SUPPORT FOR ISRAEL
- STOP TERRORIST INVASIONS

First Amendment- Religion and Expression: "Congress shall make no law respecting an establishment of religion, or prohibiting the free exercise thereof; or abridging the freedom of speech, or of the press; or the right of the people peaceably to assemble, and to petition the Government for a redress of grievances".

AN EXAMPLE OF CONFLICTING ELEMENTS

GRAYSON, Ky. — After five nights in jail for <u>refusing to issue marriage licenses</u> to same-sex couples, Kim Davis, a Kentucky county clerk, walked free Tuesday to a roar of cheers from thousands of supporters, but she and her lawyer would not sm whether she would continue to defy court orders and try to blc the licenses. Outside the jail here, a planned demonstration b) people who, like Ms. Davis, say that <u>same-sex marriage</u> violate their religious beliefs turned buoyant when she was released, t sense of triumph mixed with a dose of presidential politics.

Many legal strategist do not agree with Ms. Davis action and it as the wrong fight to pick. However, the fight will not be between those well versed in natural law and the opposition b common lay persons who are every day God fearing people we know a lot about the Bible in their Country where the Bible a Christianity is foundational. So, resistance to same sex marri is coming from many directions. We have to hold fast to what we know is right. It doesn't take a Scientist or an Anthropology to know the difference and purpose of male and female. If we don't stand for what we know is right, we will fall for anything. Reputable scholars and many learned men and women conclude that the Supreme Court has violated the constitution by maki a law involving religion...... Marriage was designed by God a sanctioned by divine authority and revelation. We support Davis to the limit. One thing she knows, same sex entanglement being called marriage is dead wrong.

THE CHURCH and SAME SEX MARRIAGE

<u>Same Sex Marriage-</u> This is a social ill with various contributory factors. The more sophisticated species in the animal kingdom (man and woman) are subject to emotion, perception and complicated inordinate affection. Unlike other species of the animal kingdom, humans are not programmed for limited cycles where the animal is in heat. Humans by virtue of the psyche are open to intuition, imagination, sensory perception, dreams and extraneous abnormal thoughts and desires. From this comes addiction, perversion, homosexuality and deception from the spirit world.

Same sex marriage is the culmination of these inner conflicts not the cause. In general all earlier societies rejected the notion that there were no prevention or cure for these abnormalities. It is not unusual that a boy may have features like his mother or a girl may have her father's features. But if the biology and the physiology is clearly distinctive, then the identity should follow suit. The identity has a lot to do with environment and parenting. Don't associate with the chickens if you don't intend to be one. Teach the child that he/she is in charge of their identity and destiny and they can do all things through Christ. The "CAN DO" message resonates far more than the "CAN'T" message. Through conditioning, many types of objects or situations can become sexually stimulating-particularly among preadolescents and adolescents-including erotic literature, sex scenes in plays and films, pictures of nude or partially nude individuals, and underclothing or other objects intimately associated with potential sexual partners. Sexual arousal may also accompany strong emotional reactions- such as fear and excitement especially if associated with the performance of some forbidden act. Consequently without defense mechanisms such as consciousness toward God and knowledge of His Word conceived in intimacy, one's mind and emotions may be carried in all directions resulting in deviant behavior. One 66 must soundly resist and reject the onslaught of deviant behavior. **Abnormal Psychology and Modern Life, Carson/Butcher and Coleman/ 1988.**

Pedophilia - Pedophilia is not pronounced very loudly but if it raises. its voice/ it is snuffed out rather quickly. There is no attempt to explain its origin or normalize its practice.

"CONTROL// is the word don/t even think about coming out of the closet.

Variant Sexual Behavior- in variant sexual behavior such as pedophilia and homosexuality/ satisfaction is dependent primarily on something other than a mutually desired sexual engagement with sexually mature members of the opposite gender. So defined/ a vast array of preference patterns are comprised in which the sexual development of the affected individual has for some reason deviated from the standard/ adult heterosexual course. This deviation has a psychological base not a biological or a physiological base. Consequently it is learned/ or thought/ or conceived from the environment whether through explicit music/ language/ pornographic pictures/ or accepted societal norms created by a fallen degenerate culture. When such negative stimuli is conceived/ it may require supernatural power to break it before it runs it1S course.

The best antidote is physical removal from the scene. Disengagement will neutralize aggressive stimuli and establish normal logical reasoning. What does the Bible say? "Then when lust hath conceived, it bringeth forth sin: and sin, when it is finished, bringeth forth death." James 1:15

You must control your thinking. Don't allow all kinds of mental garbage to be deposited in your mind. Think on these things "Finally, brothers and sisters, whatever is true, whatever is noble, whatever is right, whatever is pure, whatever is lovely, whatever is admirable--if anything is excellent or praiseworthy--think about such things". Philippians 4:8.

CONCLUSION

Same agents found in pedophilia are found in homosexuality and other deviant behaviors. Society demands that the pedophile control his deviant sexual drives and behave according to the accepted societal norms. This may be done in many ways that are not repressive. What one believes plays a major part in controlling behavior. Conceiving the positive and displacing the negative is productive and successful. Counseling can be highly instructive in shaping the kind of mental attitude desired and finding peaceful solutions where there may be conflicts.

Isn't it interesting that the one who brought peaceful solutions to mankind is JESUS CHRIST? JESUS SAID: John 14:27, " Peace I leave with you, My peace I give to you; not as the world gives do I give to you. Let not your heart be troubled, neither let it be afraid".

Peace that Jesus gives overcomes repression. Your prayer life will result in peace when coupled together with obedience to God's Word. The road to same sex marriage began with unrecognized deviant behavior. It was not treated as pedophilia is treated, was not condemned, and therefore not treated. Great conflict arises in the Church over this issue because the bible clearly openly condemns the practice of homosexuality. Neither the homosexual, nor any other person involved in deviant behavior is condemned any more than fornicators, adulterers, liars are condemned. The practice is condemned not the person. True confession and real repentance will be required by the true church in order for true fellowship and participation in the sacraments to be administered.

Churches should make sure their by-laws and job descriptions have clear language on required behavior for officers and employees and expected behavior for all members. All members are expected to persevere in the Christian walk. Churches must state clearly up front their position on same sex marr1age The Supreme Court ruling on same sex marriage does not supersede the first amendment. The church is open to the public for worship, for prayer and participation in any and all religious and social services provided by the church so long as participation is lawful, reasonable and for the right purpose. The church tax exempt status enables the church to offer services, provide food, education, counseling, temporary shelter, aid to families and many other community and family needs without racial, gender, orientation or natural origin discrimination. The church does not condone, promote, or permit practices of adultery, fornication, homosexuality or any acts of deviant behavior. The church invites and encourages all sinners to choose to come for cleansing whether involved in deviant life style, social deviance or personal sinful life style, the gospel of Jesus Christ has a strong reputation over thousands of years and millions of people of changing lives from the most depraved conditions.

A statement of the church regarding same sex marriage and any involvement therein by the church or any minister or leader of the church is that it is totally forbidden. The Episcopal Bishop has stated well the church position. "As the Episcopal Bishop of the Diocese of Rhode Island, I firmly support the traditional definition of marriage as the union between one male and one female. I believe that Holy Matrimony is a sacred religious rite, whose definition should not be re-interpreted by legislation or civil courts."

A Divine Institution. The Bible presents marriage as a divine institution. If marriage were of human origin, then human beings would have a right to decide the kind of marital relationships to choose. Marriage, however, began with God. It was established by God at the beginning of human history when He "created the heavens and the earth" (Gen-1:1). As the Creator of marriage, God has the right to tell us which principles should govern our marital relationships. If God had left us no instructions about marriage after establishing it, then marriage could be regulated according to personal whims. But He has not left us in the dark. In His revelation contained in the pages of the Bible, God has revealed His will regarding the nature and function of marriage. As Christians who choose to live in accordance with God's will, we must study and respect those Biblical principles governing marriage, divorce, and remarriage. In some instances, the laws of a state regarding marriage, divorce and remarriage ignore or even violate the teachings of the Bible. In such cases, as Christians, "we must obey God rather than men" (Acts 5:29).

Samuele Bacchiocchi, Ph. D., Andrews University

Marriage is a divine institution instituted by God and is a religious institution typical of the union between Christ and the Church. We will not violate the laws of God in order to satisfy the State or political correctness. We will not perform mock wedding ceremonies involving same sex partners Supreme Court is in violation of the first amendment

DEFENDERS OF CHURCH AND STATE

Chief Justice Roberts

Associate Justice Clearance Thomas

Justice Antonin Scalia

Justice Samuel Alito

THESE ARE THE BRAVE MEN WHOSE DEFENSE OF THE CONSTITUTION PRESERVES THE TRUE VALUE and QUALITY OF LIFE WHICH DISTINGUISHED AMERICA FROM OTHER NATIONS.

The Supreme Court ruled 5-4 that the Constitution requires that same sex couples be allowed to marry no matter where they live and that states may no longer **reserve the right only for heterosexual couples.**

Supreme Court rules gay couples nationwide have a right to marry.

Chief Justice Roberts

He delved into the history of marriage and wrote that other cases that had changed aspects of marriage - like the *Loving* case - **but none until now had changed its core structure as being between a man and a woman.** The chief justice also suggested that the logic applied by the majority to same-sex marriage might also be employed to defend polygamy, writing, "It is striking how much of the majority's reasoning would apply with equal force to the claim of a fundamental right to plural marriage."

Associate Justice Clarence Thomas

Thomas interpreted "liberty" in the due process clause of the 14th Amendment as referring specifically to "freedom from restraint." With that in mind, he wrote that the petitioners couldn't claim "under the most plausible definition of liberty,' that they have been imprisoned or physically restrained by the States for participating in same-sex relationships," noting that they have "been left alone to order their lives as they see fit."

What they had not been granted by the states is the formal recognition of their marriages in a formal way, and Thomas argued, "Liberty is only freedom from governmental action, not an entitlement to governmental benefits. "Thomas' criticism of the majority was scathing:

"Perhaps recognizing that these cases do not actually involve liberty as it has been understood, the majority goes to great lengths to assert that its decision will advance the 'dignity' of same-sex couples ... The flaw in that reasoning, of course, is that the Constitution contains no 'dignity' Clause, and even if it did, the government would be incapable of bestowing dignity." And he maintained that the court had "short-circuit[ed]" the political process by not allowing states to define marriage for themselves, and he predicted the majority's decision could have "potentially ruinous consequences for religious liberty." Marriage is a divine institution predetermined by God with permanent and specific construction based on original design of the genders for a specific purpose. The purpose and / or design is fixed with immutable specific practices which cannot be crossed without being abominable, fruitless and obnoxious.

The constitution does not require that same sex couples be allowed to marry. **FIVE JUSTICES REQUIRE THAT SAME SEX UNIONS BE RECOGNIZED.**

These are not elected men and women representing constituents and allowing the democratic process to function.

Rather the democratic process is circumvented by five justices who through judicial activism have imposed their liberalism on the represented body and deprived them of the right to be represented in this matter by their representatives which is constitutional. As Justice

Roberts has stated, no changes to marriages by the courts have ever sought to change its core structure from being between one man and one woman. What God has fixed is set in stone. It is consistent with the design. The psychology and the biology follow the design when normal function is in place. Procreation requires heterosexual attraction this attraction leads to the production of offspring. Abnormal homosexual attraction is not consistent with the design and purpose for which the design exists. Chief Justice Roberts

Continued: "The majority today relies on its own understanding of what freedom is and must become," he said to the court, and the deepest problem with their decision was "the disrespect it shows the democratic process. "With this decision, proponents of same-sex marriage lost the opportunity to win acceptance through the democratic process, he said, and "they lose this just when the winds of change were freshening at their backs."

"Five lawyers," he said, deemed themselves chosen, **"to burst the bonds of history."**

Associate Justice Antonin Scalia

Scalia mocked the majority in his dissent, calling the opinion "judicial Putsch," said that it was filled with "straining-to-be-memorable passages." He also wrote, "the opinion is couched in a style that is as pretentious as its content is egotistic.

Justice Samuel Alito

Alito stood up for marriage as tradition that goes back for millenia, saying it was "inextricably linked" to procreation.

He also wrote about religious liberty in his dissent, saying the decision "will be used to vilify Americans who are unwilling to assent to the new orthodoxy."

Rev. Appolles Sweatte wrote: (Marriage Divorce and the Believer),

Vantage Press, **1988,** "A staggering number of people today are ready to undo in a matter of weeks what was intended for life. According to reports, approximately 50 percent of the marriages formed in our modem-day society end in divorce. Yes there is something grossly wrong with our society. It has eaten the bitter herbs of humanism and drank the deadly poison of atheism. It does not have God in conscious awareness and cannot provide a climate for successful marriages. A society without morals and values cannot contribute to the success of its offspring; it is the catalyst that produces lust, sex, and divorce. A healthy marriage depends first on moral consciousness. If we are to have life proper, abundant life, full and complete, we can only derive such a life from the Master Mind. God is omniscient, omnipresent, and omnipotent. He is holy, eternal, and immutable. In order for there to be a duplication, there has to be an original. There must be a pattern to copy, a standard to measure by, a true form, a mark of perfection, a "right way" and a "wrong way". Such a design, such a high order of intelligence can only be found in God and those to whom His Word is revealed. "Man shall not live by bread alone but by the Word of God (Luke 4:4). Marriage is a divine institution, constituted at the beginning before the origin of human society.

The Creator made man male and female, and ordained marriage as the indispensable condition of the continuance of the race (Gen. 1 :27-28). He implanted social affections and desires in man's nature. He made marriage an ennobling influence powerfully contributing to the development of a complete life in man and woman. The support systems for a free society keeping it morally sound and socially just, are "God, "the family" and the "home". It is when man loses his identity with God that he becomes carnal, sensual, and devilish. The marriage suffers and the home is broken"

BUZZ WORDS and BUSINESS

Politics has coined certain buzz words which they elasticize and move in any direction so as to create a form that may be completely the opposite of the original. Such terms as "rights" "require" "gay" or certain phrase as "right to choose" while the mother has the right to choose, she takes away the baby's right to life. In the Supreme Court's majority opinion, the constitution **requires** that same sex couples be allowed to marry. And that gay. couples nationwide have the **right** to marry.

John F. Kennedy Proclaiming that rights, come not from the State, but from the hand of Almighty God. Marriage is already defined by

God. This, that the Supreme Court is authorizing is not marriage it's fake, phony, rejected by God, immoral, contributes nothing to society, introduces a foul image and a corrupt relationship which will damage children that may be involved. To say that the constitution REQUIRES this abomination shows the effect of gross elasticization. Of course these are justices the constitution says whatever they want it to say. As President John F. Kennedy

said: **"Rights come not from the State, but from the hand of the Almighty God". God has not given anyone the right to re-define marriage.**

THE CLAIM TO RIGHTS

The claim to **"rights"** finds itself in many places and with many faces. Since the successful demand for Civil Rights in the 1960's, where basic human rights were denied African Americans solely based on natural origin, on their physical being at birth without choice or right to choice regarding their physical being, every undeserving group want to claim that their deviant behavior deserves to be called a Civil Rights issue. African Americans Because they were born black were easily identified and targeted for abuse. They were stereotyped and abused. They had no closet to go in, no place to hide. They were rejected in the public square as someone with leprosy. They were pushed to the back and denied due process. Their physical lives were made a living hell. Yet they wanted to fight in the white folks army and defend the freedom they were surely to be denied. They had to fight like hell for privileges others had simply by virtue of being born Now, someone comes along, develops a deviant behavior, such as an abnormal attraction, becomes an alcoholic or drug addict, or maybe a pedophile. These practices are to be included under the umbrella of Civil Rights??? There are no rights based on the way one chooses to have sex. There are no "gay rights" the so-called gay community is protected under the 14th amendment like everybody else. Being gay, or being homosexual, or being a pedophile is not a right it's a temporary fallen state that one can overcome. There are many behavioral deficiencies some children have to overcome. The behavior is rejected and the child grows and breaks free because deviant behavior is displaced and correct behavior is assimilated. People of faith should not accept deviant behavior exemplified by their children. This society is out of concentricity with the moral code. Those with God consciousness ask the question, "what did God say?" When they know that, that becomes ground zero. Confer with your pediatrician to clear any medical conditions. If you accept the Word of God as absolute authority, you have the basis that empower you to speak with authority. The child needs your help not your pity or sympathy.

Mark 11 :22-23 "Jesus answering saith unto them: "HAVE FAITH IN GOD". For verily I say unto you, that whosoever. shall SAY unto this mountain "BE THOU REMOVED" and shall not doubt in his heart, but shall believe that those things "WHICH HE SAITH" shall come to pass, he shall have whatsoever. he saith.

a. When you pray believe that you receive and you shall have

b. When you stand praying forgive if you have ought against any that your heavenly Father may forgive you your trespasses.

The Country is greatly benefited when intangible values and qualities characterize its representatives. The Church will never die for the gates of hell shall not prevail. It is written: **"on this** rockr111 **I will build my church, and the gates of** heii£RI **shall not prevail against** it".

(Matthew 16: 17) The Day America Spurned God THE DAY THE CHURCH DENIED GOD AND BOWED TO MADELYN MURRAY O'HARA "But as for my enemies who did not want me for their king bring them here and execute them in my presence." *Luke 19:27* In June of 1963, the Supreme Court upheld the argument of the atheist Madelyn Murray O'Hare and promulgated an edict with ramifications so widespread it insured that God would be evicted from public society across the entire spectrum of the American governmental system. From that day to this, not only has prayer been outlawed, God's very name has been declared anathama to the United States Constitution, and forbidden to be mentioned in any federal, state, county, city or municipal context Further decrees have revealed the depths of the ouster that initial edict has fostered. Not just prayer is forbidden in the public forum. Display of the cross is forbidden. The Ten Commandments are forbidden. The Bible is forbidden.

Even the mere mention of the names "God" or "Jesus" in schools are forbidden. More than that, anything even suggestive of those names is forbidden. No question about it, Pharaoh's heart has changed (Exod. I4:4).

The government's legal decision hit like an earthquake when it was first delivered! Up to that moment, most people considered the United States government tantamount to a church. The morality echoed by both was virtually identical. It was that perceived union which inspired the public's reverence for its political system in the first place. Just as it is today, almost every person in the country at the time of the Court decision was Christian.

Displays of the Ten Commandments, the parables, Gospel quotations and Christian exhortations were everywhere. There were prayers in public schools, in public forums, virtually all government affairs and congress.

Public grammar schools conducted nativity plays. The morality ofthe society was Judea-Christian. Forgiveness was an essential principle in the land.

Factors other than money drove the national mind. Businesses closed their doors on Good Friday. God and Jesus were ubiquitous in almost every aspect of American society. Suddenly all that was gone. All of it purged from the American scene in one sudden ruling. That ruling was less a decision about school-sanctioned prayer than it was a decision about the constitution itself. MM O'Hare is the figurehead of this decision because she led the cause. As an atheist, she filed her petition on the grounds of separation of church and state, evoking the Constitution's own words. The reward went to atheism. There was no compromise, no blending of the past with the future. The Court agreed with her and threw God out of the public arena. For all intents and purposes, the Court ruled the U.S. Constitution a Godless document. The Godly do not even have a place in it. The atheists not only have a place in it, they now own it. The realization of that horrifying thought left much of the nation aghast.

Not only was there no place for God in the Constitution, the Court ruled there never would be. Like a baby in a custody suit, the Constitution was brought into court with MM O'Hare claiming it belonged to her instead of the Godly par ents that had been raising it for the previous 200 years. The Court examined the writing, tested it, and, in the end, said to her, 'You're right, Madeline, God has no place in this document.' So they stripped

82 out of the hands of the God-fearing people ho had been loving and nourishing it since,1776, and handed it to O'hara instead, the woman who hated God. Here it it's all yours', they said as they handed the document to its new mother. She was euphoric in her victory. The people of righteousness were dumbfounded in their grief. The court had taken the constitution out of their hands and given it to the atheist. There was no compromise. There is no place here, ruled the Court, for two mothers.

Immediately, as proof of what had just happened, God was stripped from all aspects of the government. It was a national purge. The consequences were enormous. So was the purge. Out went Christmas, the public decorations and Creche displays, the writing, the moral lessons, the Ten Commandments, the nativity plays in schools, and on and on and on. The word "God" had suddenly become anathema in the public forum and was stripped away as if it were as incendiary as a Communist call to arms.

There were many subsequent decisions, but the court never wavered in its initial assessment. The purge was relentless. It was the first in a series of decisions the Supreme Court issued deciding God's place in our system of government. They ruled He had no place in our constitution, and therefore no place in our governmental society. They made God the forbidden fruit of the nation. His name could not be mentioned in the public forum, His Son's name could not be mentioned, nor could His words or commandments be seen or discussed, especially by the nation's school children. Today, 40 years later, we see the corporate and media worlds joining forces with the government to expand the purge to the very limits of the national society. So deadly is the idea of God to our Court that Karl Marx can be mentioned and Marx's words can be taught, but not Christ's. A Lyric by John Lennon can hang in a courthouse, but not the Ten Commandments. With heads spinning the people have tried to comprehend this seemingly illogical interpretation concerning separation of church and state. How could it be twisted to mean the expulsion of God from the American public arena? How could it be used to shred our former way of life and strip it naked of Diety? How could it mean the word "God" was now a forbidden term in public school or any other government institution? How could It come to mean an historic cross microscopically hidden in a crowded county seal had to be expunged? My own thinking is that the Court made a mistake. Either they were incompetent or they used a faulty test when they made their examination and ruled the 83

Constitution a document for atheists only. I think the opinion needs to be readdressed and ruled on again. It seems to me unconscionable that our country has been mandated to atheism by our own judiciary. There must be room for the presence and mention of God in school and in the public forum, just as there is room for being anti-God. When the WW-11 Memorial was erected recently in Washington D.C., a quotation by Franklin Delano Roosevelt, was altered to purge his phrase "so help me God" from the plaque. Because of the Supreme Court's knee-jerk response to MM O'Hare, godlessness is now the nation's highest principle. When 90% of the U.S. population is religious and 85% of it Christian, that is an egregious error begging to be corrected as quickly as possible. What are the consequences for spuming God? Does this separation between God and government remove the shield of Grace that has guarded our country since its inception? If so, what can we expect? Did God send us any warning, any sign? Five months after the American Supreme Court expelled Jesus, the president of the United States was assassinated. John Kennedy fell to an assassin's bullet in Dallas, Texas. Just months after that Johnson plunged the United States into the Vietnam War. Using the Gulf of Tonkin as an excuse, he ordered 400,000 troops sent into VietNam to replace the 15,000 American 'Advisors' who were there when he became president. The war he pushed lasted ten years and killed, maimed or wounded over 200,000 Americans. What had the prophecies warned? Assassination, wars, earthquake and tidal wave? Exactly nine months after the Supreme Court ruling. the final signs were delivered on Good Friday, the anniversary of the Lord's crucifixion. On that day, in April of 1964 the United States suffered its worst earthquake and tidal wave in recorded history, a 9.2 behemoth that shattered Alaska and sent massive tidal waves roaring across the Pacific coastline, obliterating towns all across Alaska before smashing its way southward destroying cities all the way to the port of Los Angeles where, even in that distant city, it inflicted more than a hundred thousand dollars in damages. But all that was just the warning. An earthquake on Good Friday would seem, itself, a sign. In the ninth hour, just after 3 PM, when Jesus died on the cross, the veil of the Temple was tom in two from top to bottom, and an earthquake split the rocks. "Meanwhile, the centurion, together with the others guarding Jesus, had seen the earthquake and all that was taking place, and they were terrified and said, 'In truth this was the son of God." (Mat.27:54).In Bible chronology, the Good Friday earthquake and its tidal waves in America occurred in the eleventh hour (just after 5 PM), during the ninth hour of Alaskan daylight A sign? If so, coming just nine months after America had removed God from its government, it seemed also a signal of the lateness of the world's hour. Roget's Thesaurus calls the eleventh hour the "crucial moment, the critical moment, the decisive moment, the moment of truth; the psychological moment; the nick of time; the zero hour, the H hour, D day, the deadline." Was the Madelyn Murray O'Hare ruling America's moment of truth? Did it (over a period of nine months) give birth to a stream of fateful proofs? Are we racing now against a deadline set by God? Was that Supreme Court decision the zero hour for our country? Scripture says yes to all of these. The Bible tells us the denial of God is always fatal. According to scripture, America and the other nations of the western world, by removing God from the master/heads of their stately ships, have struck off on a course to oblivion.

Ignoring the warnings and refusing to repent it's decision to governmentally abandon God, our nation has steadily enlarged the gap between itself and safety. We can only conclude that the "Great Revolt" Paul predicted (2 Thes.2:3) has now taken place and even the United States has succumbed to its influence. For this reason, it is important that we examine the signs and become cognizant of the events that scripture has declared will precede and accompany the "day of vengeance" made manifest by the rebellion. The most obvious of these signs are the very ones which followed the Supreme Court's 1963 decision, i.e., assassination (Jer.44:29- 30), earthquake (Mat.24:7), warfare (Mat.24:6) and tidal wave (Jer.51:42). These seem to be the most important in terms of the Revolt and its consequences, but there are many more. Jesus tells us there will be signs in the sun and moon and stars. We can expect to see lawlessness so virulent that love on earth will virtually disappear. Worldwide distress beyond anything ever seen before will follow in its wake. There will be widespread famine; even cosmic "hailstones". All of this because the world has rejected and spumed Christ's offer of peace. The denial of God brings catastrophe. That is what the signs all point to. The separation of America from God guarantees, not justice, only trouble. It removes the shield of grace that protects our nation from the assaults of Satan and nature. Unless our government reverses its fateful course, our nation seems certain to have to participate in the mechanism of God's Judgment. That has already been made evident. In 2001, God made our nation the billboard announcing His day of vengeance. On September 11th, of that year, 38 years after the Supreme Court's decision on O'Hare's petition was declared the law of the land, the images of the 18th chapter of the Book of Revelation were written on the walls of America's city towers. The world is Babylon and America has become the world's policeman. That makes America the world's wall the nations' first line of defense against attack. We didn't want to be, but God has forced us against our will to become the wall of Babylon. That is why 9/11 was so fateful. God was able to display Revelation's fateful chapter before the eyes of the whole world in a sure sign of the certain fate that lies ahead. According to Jeremiah, the definitive biblical proof of the attack and military presence of foreign troops in Jerusalem will be displayed before the eyes of all mankind in the assassination of the "Pharaoh of Egypt" (Jer.44:29-30). It is this attack that the Book of Revelation discuses in terms of the drying up of the Euphrates river (Rev. 16: 12) (Rev. 9: 14-19). If that catastrophic event is accompanied by an earthquake and the tidal waves against the coasts of Babylon so widely prophesied, it will bring us full circle back to 1963 Scripture tells us that the world has been living the past 2000 years in a "year of favor" from God. It is called the "millennium" because scripture tells us a year to God is like a thousand years to man. God has almost doubled that period of world grace, just as Joshua said He would (Josh. lO: 12-15). Jesus began His ministry by standing up in a synagogue in Nazareth and reading words from a text by the prophet Isaiah. The text of His reading concerned the "year of favor" that has produced the rule of Christ on earth for the last 20 centuries God's offer of peace to the world. Jesus told the congregation listening to Him that Isaiah's words were about Himself and that they were being fulfilled in their hearing: The spirit of the Lord God has been given to *me,* for God has anointed me.

He has sent me to bring good news to the poor, to bind up hearts that are broken; to proclaim liberty to captives, freedom to those in prison; to proclaim a year of favor from the Lord, a day of vengeance for our God . " (Is.61:1-2). For almost 2000 years historians have revealed a world bathed in the Gospel of Christ through the active encouragement of western governments. God's year of favor became a hundred years and then a thousand years and then another thousand. Century after century, Satan's captives all over the earth were set free and led to safety by the cross of Christ. Assisted in their flight by the governments of the world, the journey of God's people from this world to the next was made easier by those who ruled them with God in mind.

Only in the last 1 00 years has world encouragement seriously faltered. First evident in Europe, we have watched an astonishing reversal of the western world's support of Jesus since then. Although last in the list of governments to denounce Him, nowhere in the world has the official denial of God been more dramatically and clearly stated than in the United States of America, thanks not only to MM O'Hare, but to all the government officials, politicians and judges who flocked to her side, leaving Jesus standing alone.

The rule of Christ was first created on earth when the Roman Empire ordered the purge of Godlessness from its empire and put God in charge of its government. Our Supreme Court has done exactly the reverse. They have overturned all that Constantine, Theodosius and Galerius emplaced. Now it is God who is being purged from the government and Godlessness championed in His place.

Scripture warns that God's year of favor will end (and the day of vengeance begin) when Christ's offer of reconciliation is spumed by a revolt of the people and their governments (John 3:19). Yet prophecy predicts that is the very thing they will do throw off his rule and toss Him and His words out of their hearing (2 Thes.2:3).

Prophecy is clear. That revolt brings the tribulation and the Judgment. Goodnews Christian Ministry http://goodnewspirit.com

BOTH THE CHURCH and THE STATE HAS FAILED GOD
THE FAILURE OF THE CHURCH

In preference church harvest is supplied by the home. Children properly trained become excellent leader material for setting examples for proper character and conduct. Having been built on a foundation of self adjustment derived from biblical principles and true faith in God. American families of yesteryear valued the bible as a valuable integral part of their lives which contributed not only to the success of the family, but impact the neighborhood, community, city, state and the whole country. Political leaders shine brighter when they are fueled by the flame of moral justice. Much of the Christian communities are deceived by the statement: "separation of church and state. It has been used to condemn prayer and bible reading in schools where it's desperately needed. Studies will show how much violence, wickedness, shootings in schools and public places has increased without emphatic moral guidance. Faith plays an integral part in one's life. It does matter what one believes. One's self talk will direct one in the right way when that self-talk is based in TRUTH. What Truth?? JESUS SAID: I AM THE TRUTH: (jn 14:6) JESUS IS THE ESSENCE OF TRUTH. You can trust what He says. You can trust what He does. There is no guile or negativity found in Him. HE IS LORD! This answers the question of absoluteness. He is absolutely real. YOU ARE HIS CREATION. HE IS TRUE IN LIFE, DEATH, AND RESURRECTION. HE SAID IT, HE DID IT and HE'S ALIVE TO PROVE IT IN US.

SEPARATION OF CHURCH and STATE

There's a huge misunderstanding that somehow the First Amendment places a "wall of separation" between church and state – an unfortunate phrase used by Thomas Jefferson in a letter to the Danbury Baptist Association, in Connecticut. To deliberately mix metaphors, the "wall of separation" has been used as a sledgehammer, especially in recent years, against churches and people of faith. While some complain that the so-called "wall of separation" is crumbling, the truth is it has grown thicker and higher over the decades, threatening to crush our first freedom.

The phrase is not found in the Constitution, nor is it in the Bill of Rights. If the Founders had wanted to, they could easily have included a "wall of separation." But as University of Chicago's Professor of Law Philip Hamburger argues in *Separation of Church and State* they strove to create something new: real religious liberty, without state overreach and control. They said that Congress could not establish a national church, nor could it prohibit the free exercise of religion.

And that "free exercise of religion" isn't just about "private worship" or "individualized faith," it includes the freedom of individuals and different faiths to exercise belief and conviction in the public arena through their speech and actions. Any wall of separation constructed between government and church was made of perishable material. There was no restrictions put on the CHURCH which is (A BODY OF BAPTIZED BELIEVERS) The State wasn't trying to monitor or regulate prayer and worship, it was power, authority and money that the government would control. The antichrist and the atheist who are inspired by satan saw this as an opportunity to raise an apparent objection. The church is assigned to a KINGDOM that is not of this world that is a SPIRITUAL KINGDOM and is not subject to the kingdoms of this world except by divine order. The church would like for the government to join us in prayer as was the practice of the founding fathers however, the church will not seek permission from the government to pray. The voice of morality is demonstrated by the church triumphant or members of the body who have the victory. NO ONE CAN STOP YOU FROM PRAYING ANYWHERE. Faith, character and Content so desperately needed in leadership is derived from knowledge of the truth. "You shall know the truth and the truth shall make you free. John 8:32. Unfortunately many, many pastors drank the kool-aid of the "separation of church and state doctrine and refused to occupy and resist and stand up against Madolyn Ohara and not let one person stop the whole country from exercising the constitutional right to religious freedom. Christians should have been involved in that decision not to enforce prayer in school but demonstrate their right to be heard. In all probability the decision would have been one to accommodate both sides. sides. Failure of the church to fulfill its call to be salt and light and to offer resistance against the evil that has crept into our country John 17. Sexual sins and deviant behavior once considered abnormal are now accepted as normal. It wasn't enough to have men with men and women with women, satan would corrupt minds further with transgender corruption (Romans 1.) THESE ARE ALL

MIND DISEASES. For the most part the church acquiesce and find ways to justify and tolerate ungodly practices. THERE ARE ONLY A FEW VOICES CONDEMNING THESEUNGODLY PRACTICES.

MIND DISEASES MUST BE HANDLED BY THE CHURCH

It is critical that the church has the Spirit of the Lord. Ritual and custom and tradition has its place but it cannot help with special needs. Spiritual phenomena respond to spiritual dynamics. Jesus said: "you shall receive power after that the holy ghost (Spirit of God), comes upon you and you shall be a powerful witness. (Acts 1:8) God has full control over the spirit world. See Samuel 10:6 "The Spirit of the Lord will come upon you, and you shall prophesy with the prophets AND SHALL BE TURNED INTO ANOTHER MAN". True believers have been turned into another man or woman or have become new creatures in Christ. (2Corinthians 5:17) WARNING

The Spirit of the Lord departed from Saul, and an evil spirit from the Lord troubled him (1Samuel 16:14). Saul's dilemma came because of disobedience. To obey is better than sacrifice and to hearken than the fat of rams". (1Samuel 15:22). BEING IN THE PRESENCE OF THE SPIRIT OF GOD, BEING AROUND PEOPLE WHO ARE FILLED WITH THE SPIRIT OF GOD, HEARING THE WORD OF THE SPIRIT OF GOD, FOLLOWING TEACHINGS OF THE SPIRIT OF GOD, BEING FILLEED WITH THE SPIRIT OF GOD, BEING BAPTIZEED IN THE SPIRIT OF GOD, IS A STRONG DEFENSE.

1. Results in a sound mind and true identity
2. Makes one whole, body mind and spirit
3. Free from gender confusion
4. Not easily persuaded to believe a lie
5. Able to discern between good and evil

1. Parents are empowered to convince their children of true identity. Teach them: don't let the devil teach them.
2. You have the Word of God as blessed assurance.

THE CHURCH ADOPTED SEVERAL DESTRUCTIVE PRACTICES AND BEHAVIORS OF THE WORLD.

The Evis Presley Style does not belong in the Church. It is understandable that young people will go for hot rock But through development understanding and spiritual growth, a new reality will be realized as the new creature In Christ surfaces with a new mind. Therefore if any man or woman, boy or girl be in CHRIST, he or she is a NEW CREATURE old things are passed away behold all things have become new (2Corinthians 5:17). THIS MAY BE RECOGNIZED AS THE NEW BEGINNING OF THE SEX REVOLUTION. Characterized by finger-popping, butt slinging and knee-jerking fueled by pot, coke, heroin and other mind-altering drugs. The church is surrounded by moral decadence disorder and disrespect for dignity. Unfortunately the church is impacted by the world and the world's music. The pull of the Holy Spirit draws one vertically more ostensibly toward the image of Christ. The Church presents the voice of the angels not the cry for love lost or love sought. The beat of the drums and the sound of the guitar do not call for sexual encounter but rather ring out for joy and excitement because of victory over drug addiction, perverted sexual habits, convoluted entanglements with polluted relationships, and truly no peace. The church must lead our young people to Jesus, the prince of peace. THERE IS NO KNOWLEDGE WITHOUT EXPERIENCE. YOU KNOW BY PERNAL ENCOUNTER. When you ask a question you know when you get an answer. When you ask the Lord to save you, you will know emphatically that you were heard, CHANGE TAKES PLACE. You are the first to know that something has happened and you are different. No doubt you will hear testimonies of many of those you know who share their experience. IT IS NOT RELIGION, IT'S RELATIONSHIP. You do things different from the world because you have a new mind. You think different, you look different, you dress different, you walk different. Your value system changes you are separate from the world and the world knows there is a great change in you. Jesus asked His disciples: "who do you say I am{? " Peter answered: " You are the Christ" Jesus said to Peter, God has revealed this knowledge to you it didn't come from natural means. You don't really know until God reveals His Son Jesus to you as your Savior then you have a testimony and you want to tell everyone.

THE CHURCH SHOULD TAKE THE LEAD IN MORAL EXCELLENCE SO-CALLED SEPARATION OF CHURCH AND STATE IS NOT A CONSTITUTIONAL DOCTRINE.

The constitution does not prevent the free exercise of accepted Christian practices regarding speech and reasonable performance of Christian duties. It must be realized that our country is largely built on Christian Doctrine. As long as we adhere to basic fundamental biblical principles and values in practice since the Pilgrim's progress, we will stand. Quiet to the contrary, if we continue to dismantle principles and biblical mandates and disregard moral laws, America will go down like the Titanic.

THE STATE HAS FAILED GOD

Yes, the State has failed God. The main area where the State or Politicians have failed is : "<u>COMMON SENSE.</u> It is so obvious that for the most part Congressmen and Senators are followers not leaders. When you are following the crowd, you are not following knowledge. POLITICIANS NEED THE WISDOM OF THE WORD. "The wicked shall be turned into hell, And all the nations that forget God" (Psalms 9:17-20). Those whom are chosen to lead should take a vital interest in making sure their constituents don't forget the values and virtues that make a home a home, makes a neighborhood viable and makes a community great. By and large we are a Christian nation. What the country is looking for is the return of Christian values. Goodness and kindness works everywhere. At home, at school, on the job, in relationships, in congress, in the senate. Jesus taught that we should love everybody. That means members of various religions, races, colors or creeds "GOD SO LOVED THE WORLD. That LOVE is absolute, without limit, comprehensive and life giving. We have this America because God gives us GRACE. THE PILGRIMS demonstrated God's favor in their voyage to the new world.

Text of The Mayflower Compact

The full text of the Mayflower Compact is as follows:

In the name of God, Amen. We, whose names are underwritten, the Loyal Subjects of our dread Sovereign Lord King James, by the Grace of God, of Great Britain, France, and Ireland, King, defender of the Faith, etc.:

Having undertaken, for the Glory of God, and advancements of the Christian faith, and the honor of our King and Country, a voyage to plant the first colony in the Northern parts of Virginia; do by these presents, solemnly and mutually, in the presence of God, and one another; covenant and combine ourselves together into a civil body politic; for our

82 better ordering, and preservation and furtherance of the ends aforesaid; and by virtue hereof to enact, constitute, and frame, such just and equal laws, ordinances, acts, constitutions, and offices, from time to time, as shall be thought most meet and convenient for the general good of the colony; unto which we promise all due submission and obedience.

In witness whereof we have hereunto subscribed our names at Cape Cod the 11th of November, in the year of the reign of our dread Sovereign Lord King James, of England, France, and Ireland, the eighteenth, and of Scotland the fifty-fourth, 1620.

For more than 150 years before a constitution was ratified the BIBLE was the guide for faith and practice. It was good for home, school, the workplace, society, community, business and family. The military, corporations and religious order found solace all these years. Through growth, education, advanced learning, through slavery, trial and error, success and failure, promise, practice and propriety. The bible inspired every discipline and established respectful norms. Every home had a bible. Children learned to believe God. Their consciousness of God as the creator with unlimited power raised a level of resistance against foolish ideas as being from the devil. They learn that Jesus loves little children and that they can talk to Him about their little problems even if mom and dad seem not to understand. The Colonies realized the need for bible education and proper interpretation of the scripture. The bible was taught in elementary school. Lesson plans were made from the scriptures. HOW DO YOU THINK WE GOT HERE? HOW DID WE BECOME EXCEPTIONAL? Our forefathers taught us and we valued the Word of God. It is not so much religion as it is relationship. Discovering and knowing the TRUTH. Knowing the TRUE life, (what's done) TRUE LOVE (what's real), TRUE SPIRIT, (what's alive). You shall know the truth because there is a truth to know. JESUS SAID: "I am the WAY the TRUTH and the LIFE (JN 14:6) THE BIBLE IS GREATER THAN THE CONSTITUTION. NOTHING THAT THE BIBLE CONDEMNS CAN BE PRACTICED IN SOCIETY WITHOUT CONSEQUENCES. Violation of moral laws will not escape judgment based on what you know. Many politicians attended Sunday school growing up and that foundation distinguishes them from unbelievers. People who do not have this foundation are more open to making foolish decisions and supporting Anti-American and Anti-God choices. Arabs who were taught to fly the planes into the world Trade Towers should have never been allowed training. You learned why in Sunday School. People who were not born in this country should not be allowed to hold government office without extreme qualifications, one of which, they can't be anti-Christian. THE STATE FAILED TO STAND FOR MORAL LAWS. CONDONATION OF EGREGIOUS SINS: SAME SEX MARRIAGE, ABORTION, MUTILATING LITTLE CHILDREN WHO ARE CONFUSED AND NEED STRONG DIRECTION FROM THEIR PARENTS IS A REAL PROBLEM.

WHEN YOU DO NOT HAVE FUNDAMENTALLY SOUND BELIEFS, YOU ARE SUBJECT TO DOING FOOLISH THINGS. WHEN THE CHILD IS OLD ENOUGH TO CONTROL HIS/HER THINKING AND REALIZE WHAT THEIR PARENTS HAVE DONE, IT COULD REALLY END IN TRAGEDY DON'T DO THIS TO YOUR CHILD TRUST GOD THE CREATOR TO GUIDE YOUR CHILD TO NORMALCY. THIS IS A SPIRITUAL ENCOUNTER NOT ANATOMICAL OR BIOLOGICAL THE MIND CONTROLS THE BODY. FIX THE MIND AND YOU WILL FIX THE BODY. WE DID NOT HAVE THIS 40/50 YEARS AGO OR IT WAS REJECTED, RESISTED OR DENIED. THERE ARE MANY TESTIMONIES OF VICTORY OVER THIS DEVIANT BEHAVIOR. WHERE IS THE COUNTRY GOING?? IF WE LISTEN TO THE LEFT, IT'S GOING TO HELL.

OUR COUNTRY HAS LOST IT'S ANCHOR

If you are not anchored, you will be dragged through the mud and fall into every pot hole. RACISM, ANTI-SEMITISM, DRUGS, CHARACTER DEFECTS, UNREASONABLE, NOT TEACHABLE, UNGODLY, WICKEDNESS, PERSONALITY FLAWS, PEDOPHILIA, GIVEN TO DEVIANCE IN MANY AREAS ETC. This group and hundreds of others require adjustment in order to become a model citizen. 'FAMILY VALUES' ARE CRITICAL. Children will be anchored at home. GOD ANCHORS THE FAMILY AND THE FAMILY ANCHORS THE CHILDREN. THE SOURCE FOR DIRECTION, INSTRUCTION AND TRAINING COMES FROM THE BIBLE RIGHTLY DIVIDED. Family beliefs are passed on to the children. It is important that TRUTH and JUSTICE are taught. Out of this web comes lawyers, judges, congressmen, senators and the whole government. ANCHORING PRINCIPLES ARE BASED ON BELIEFS OR FAITH. HERE ARE SOME BASIC PRINCIPLES THAT CHILDREN SHOULD LEARN REAL EARLY:

INSPIRED WORDS CAN ANCHOR THE MIND OF A CHILD AND GIVE THE CHILD POSITIVE DIRECTION. YES, JESUS LOVES ME AND BECAUSE HE BELIEVES IN ME, I NOW BELIEVE IN MYSELF. I AM HAPPY AND COMPLETE I HAVE VICTORY AND NOT DEFEAT. CONTINUE WITH POSITIVE CONFESSIONS AND YOU WILL HAVE POWER TO WIN EVERY BATTLE. TRANSGENDER CONFUSION IS OF THE DEVIL YOU NEED TO RESIST HIM.

YOU ARE ANCHORED IN THE WORD OF GOD YOU HAVE GOOD CONTROL. PARENTS READ THE PSALMS WITH THE CHILDREN: PSALMS: 23, 24,, 25, 27, 34, 37, AND MANY OTHERS. READ ST. JOHN. READ THE GOSPELS. ONLY THOSE CITIZENS WHO ARE ANCHORED BECAUSE THEY WERE PROPERLY TRAINED IN EARLY CHILDHOOD TO BUILD ON THE SOLID FOUNDATION AS THE FOUNDING FATHERS BUILT ON JESUS CHJRIST. GOVERNMENT SHIOULD SET BOUNDARIES OR RECOGNIZE THOSE BOUNDARIES SET BY MORAL LAW:

1. **THE TEN COMMANDMENTS SHOULD BE POSTED IN SCHOOLS, HOIMES AND CHURCHES**

2. **THE EXPECTANCY OF RESPECT BECAUSE OF LOVE FOR ONE'S NEIGHBOR MUST BE TAUGHT**

3. **PARENTS, TEACHERS, LEADERS, EVERYONE SHOULD DEMONSTRATE RESPECT FOR THE WORD OF GOD.**

4. **WE HAVE THE GREATEST CONSTITUTION BECAUSE IT IS BASED ON THE WORD OF GOD. OUR BIBLICAL FAITH IS DESIGNED FOR ALL PEOPLE. GEORGE WASHINGTON SAID IT TAKES RELIGION TO PRACTICE AND OPERATE WITH THE BONDS OF THE CONSTITUTION.**

5. **WE DO STRUGGLE WITH SOME THINGS THAT ARE FORBIDDEN BY THE BIBLE.THOSE THINGS THAT ARE FORBIDDEN ARE WITHOUT**

EXCEPTION DETRIMENTAL AND DESTRUCTIVE TO HUMAN LIFE. THOSE WHO KINOW THEY ARE WRONG BUT INSIST ON PERSUADING OTHERS ESPECIALLY CHILDREN WILL PAY A TREMENDOUS PRICE. SOME THINGS THAT STAND OUT AS EGREGIOUS ARE: A. SAME SEX MARRIAGE (STATE CONDONED) B. ALL SEXUAL SINS: RAPE, INCEST, HOMOSEXUALITY TRANSGENDERISM DECEPTION: THESE ARE MIND DISEASES MOST CASES HAVE AN EVIL SPIRIT CONNECTION. THE ESSENCE OF THIS DILEMMA IS THE FACT THAT VICTIMS ARE UNDER STRONG PERSUASION WHERE THEY BELIEVE THE LIE ABOUT THEIR BODY.

6. THIS PHENOMENA AFFECTS LITTLE CHILDREN WHO ARE CAPTIVATED BY THEIR ENVIRONMENT.

7. MOM! DAD!: "IF YOU HAVE FAITH AS A GRAIN OF MUSTARD SEED YOU CAN SAY TO THIS MOUNTAIN MOVE! MOVE! MOVE! BY THE POWER OF JESUS' NAME, IT WILL OBEY YOU. (MARK 11:23).

ABORTION DISTORTION: ABORTION HAS NOTHING TO DO WITH REPRODUCTIVE HEALTH.

IT IS A FACT THAT IN THIS DISTORTION OF THE TRUTH, AN UNBORN BABY WITH A HEART BEAT AND PARTIAL DEVELOPMENT DIES. IS IT TO SAVE THE LIFE OF THE MOTHER? NO DOUBT MORE THAN 95% OF THE TIME IT IS NOT. **WHAT MAKES ABORTION SUCH A HIGH PRIORITY??? WHY IS THE PRESIDENT SO BENT ON KILLING BABIES????? WELL, WE KNOW THE PRESIDENT IS CONCERNED ABOUT WOMENS VOTE NOT WOMEN'S HEALTH. WHAT MAKES ABORTION SO CRUCIAL? (1) THE YOUNG LADY'S SOCIAL LIFE, GOALS AND CAREER MAY BE INTERRUPTED WHILE THE YOUNG MAN FEELS NO PAIN AND IS FREE TO CORRUPT ANOTER LIFE. PRACTICE OF MORAL LAWS WOULD PREVENT THIS. CONGRESS RECOGNIZED THE NEED FOR ABSTINENCE EDUCATION IN SEX EDUCATION PROGRAM UNDER SEC. 510. {42 U.S.C. 710} (a) These** standards should be strategically taught early. Celibacy may rightly be a choice that must be respected. Thou shall not commit adultery and / or fornication along with all other "THOU SHALL NOTS" MUST

BE VIGOROUSLY TAUGHT MAINLY AT HOME. THE MALE POPULATION MUST BE TAUGHT AND REMINDED REPEATEDLY OF THE FACT THAT CHOICES HAVE CONSEQUENCES. THE PRODUCT OF THE SEED YOU PLANT IS YOUR RESPONSIBILITY. MANY WHO COME FROM FATHERLESS HOMES KNOW WHAT THIS MEANS. WHAT DOES THE BIBLE SAY ABOUT THAT? "IF ANY PROVIDE NOT FOR HIS OWN ESPECIALLY FOR THOSE OF HIS OWN HOUSE, HE HAS DENIED THE FAITH AND IS WORSE THAN AN INFIDEL (1TIMOTHY 1:1) IT IS WORTH WHILE TO PREVENT OUT OF WEDLOCK PREGNACY AND THE NEED FOR ABORTION. BOTH PARTIES OF A RELATIONSHIP SHOULD SET BOUNDARIES FROM THE BEGINNING TO PREVENT PREGNANCY.THIS WOULD BE AN ACT OF LOVE. OF COURSE IF YOU FOLLOW THE BIBLICAL MANDATE AND ABSTAIN UNTIL MARRIAGE, THIS WOULD DEMONSTRATE SELF CONTROL BY THE GRACE OF GOD. THOSE WHO ARE IN CHRIST AND WHO ARE FILLED WITH HIS SPIRIT FIND SUPERNATURAL HELP TO WALK IN VICTORY. MIND OVER MATTER MEANS FLESH UNDER SUBJECTION. EARLY INTERVENTION AND PREPARATION IS CRITICAL. THE EXAMPLE SET BY THE CHRISTIAN FAMILY STARTS ADMINISTERING TECHNIQUES FROM KINDERGARTEN AGE. CHILDREN NEED HELP, THEY NEED TRAINING THEY HAVE TO LEARN PROPER MANNERS IN RELATIONSHIPS, HOW TO DRESS, HOW TO TALK, HOW TO RESPECT SELF AND OTHERS. "BE IMITATORS OF GOD BELOVED CHILDREN AND WALK IN LOVE. LOVE PUTS GOD FIRST. WALKING IN LOVE MEANS WALKING IN OBEDIENCE TO GOD'S WORD.

ON THE ROAD TO A SOUND MIND
PSYCHOLOGY OF ADJUSTMENT

There are those who will find that they are unable and / or are unwilling to control self. Being overwhelmed by a sexually charged environment and social media charged with illicit sex, pornography and perversion, The church needs to take a hard look at it's role in society regarding moral law. Jesus said you are the salt of the earth. The ones who have the voice to instruct and teach is the CHURCH. Children who are not from a Christian home, who have not been anchored in "SELF PRESERVATION TRAINING" are vulnerable. Words are powerful and learning is critical. Parents must influence their children and teach strong principles. Deuteronomy chapter 6 sets forth a model for intense training. THE WORD OF GOD MUST BE IN THE HEART OF THE PARENTS. "These words (the bible) which I command you this day must be in your heart. You shall teach them diligently unto your children and shall talk of them when you are sitting in the house and when walking by the way, and when you lie down and when you rise". "MY SON; MY DAUGHTER. LET THEM HEAR THIS AFFIRMATION. Parents are the primary source for building sound bodies and sound minds Children must learn to live with a purpose, a plan, and goals. They must feel good about themselves. At the same time, they must know the TRUTH. HE/SHE must conform to the image God gave them. IT DOES MATTER WHAT YOU KNOW. In the Genesis account in Genesis 3:11 Adam and Eve did not know they were naked. The elevated mind was more God conscious than self conscious. They would learn that contact with the higher intelligence would give them knowledge and power. With the power of the RHEMA WORD they will reorder things in the physical world. Now that Adam and Eve are in the physical world, their growth and development will be based on learning. From day one practically all motions and movement are based on learning. Their environment consists of the physical world for what may be provided for survival. Families will learn arts and crafts that enable them to produce necessary useful products used for gardening, fishing and hunting for food and for their defense and family needs. They also had to learn about their personal growth and development. Biology and Psychology would be interesting subjects in their world. They would learn the truth about reproduction, introjection, gestation and all the stages of a pregnancy. A CHILD IS DELIVERED The child can't walk, can't talk, can't control body functions, has no knowledge of the new world he or she is born into. From here throughout, whatever he or she does, will be as, the results of learning. The child will learn to walk, talk, think, reason, tell lies, resist, knows the difference between mom and dad, learns the difference between hot and cold, knows the difference between the use of the hands and the use of the feet. The boy child quickly learns the differences between him and his little sister. You are given a child with a mind considered a "blank slate". HE OR SHE MUST NOT BE DEPRIVED OF "PROPER ATTENTION". Balanced diet for proper healthy growth is a given necessity. Deprivation may be realized more in the non-physical area such as emotions, identity, self perception, personality complex etc. Early childhood stages from infancy are critical. Parents should be diligent and introspective realizing that they are teaching and programming their child in both physical and mental growth. Although the surrounding environment will impact their experience, parental authority and training will prevail. Parents are the ones to teach proper social interacting, personhood, true identity and appreciation for God given life. Reinforce their true identity. Lead the child according to his or her innate pre-direction. (proverbs 22:6).

"All the psychosocial viewpoints on abnormal behavior focus attention in one way or another on the behavioral tendencies the child acquires in the course of early social interaction with others…. chiefly parents or parent surrogates. While their explanations vary considerably, as we have seen, all the viewpoints accept the general principle that certain deviations in parenting can have profound effects on the child's subsequent ability to cope with life's various challenges. It should be noted that a parent-child relationship is always bidirectional. The behavior of each person effects the behavior of the other" (Abnormal Psychology and Modern Life, ROBERT C. CARSON, 1988)

DEVIATION BEGINS IN THE MIND

There is great truth to be explored in both the Spiritual and the Psychological. It has been reported as fact that patients who have association with prayer even when there is some distant prayer warriors engaged, medical science has recognized a direct positive connection with these patients as opposed to those not associated with prayer. Parents are admonished to pray and teach and lead the child instead of following the immature child. When you are fine, the child will be fine. "Since personality differentiation in childhood is not as advanced as in adolescence or adulthood, children do not have as clear-cut a view of themselves and their world as they will have at a later age". They have less self-understanding and have not yet developed a stable sense of identity and an adequate frame of reference regarding reality, possibility, and value. (CARSON BUTCHER and COLEMAN, 1988)

If you are not anchored in absolute truth, you can't roar like a LION. When you are anchored in Faith, your words have power and authority. Children who have learned to be dissatisfied with their identity are going through a temporary stage of adjustment. Contact with the authority of HIM who made us will break the power of 90 deception. How one sees oneself may depend largely on what feedback is displayed, goals and achievements, overcoming objects, accolade's from friends, affirmation from parents and teachers. The child must know that he or she always has a friend they can trust in Jesus as a true friend. Parents ability to satisfy all demands will be limited. Parents do not have the capacity to address all physical, emotional, and psychological needs aside and apart from divine help, but mom and dad and the child can do all things through CHRIST who will strengthen them. "HE KNOWS". God said: " Before I formed you in the belly I knew you and before you came forth out of the womb I sanctified you and ordained you (Jeremiah 1:5). I know the thoughts that I think toward you says the Lord, thoughts of peace, and not of evil, to give you an expected end. ye shall call upon me, and ye shall go and pray unto me, and I will hearken unto you. (Jeremiah 29:11-12). OUR COUNTRY HAS ALL THIS GREATNESS AND LONGEVITY BECAUSE OF THE GRACE OF GOD. NO CONFUSION WITH GENDER, IDENTITY CRISIS, PERSONALITY DISORDER, OUT OF CONTROL SEX MANIA AND SATANIC VERSES. THIS HAS COME TO AMERICA BECAUSE AMERICA HAS DENIED CHRIST AND IN LARGE MANNER TURNED THE COUNTRY OVER TO SATAN. AMERICA HAS HEAPED TO HERSELF WICKEDNESS AND EVILL. THE ONLY OUT IS FOUND IN 2CHRONICLES 2:14. Our founding fathers set this great nation upon the twin towers of RELIGION and MORALITY. George Washington said: anyone who would attack these towers could not possibly consider themselves to be a loyal American. When we violate the principles of Faith and Godliness, we invite the wrath of God. AMERICA IS AT THE BREAKING POINT. THE DEMOCRATIC PARTY EMBRACES ALL THE THINGS THAT GOD HATES: ABORTION, TRANSGENDER CORRUPTION, SAME SEX CORRUPTION, A PRESIDENT THAT IS ANXIOUS TO LEGALIZE ABORTION IN THE NAME OF REPRODUCTIVE HEALTH. THAT MEANS THE BABY DIES. GOD HAS THE LAST SAY: "THE WICKED SHALL BE TURNED INTO HELL AND ALL THE NATIONS THAT FORGET GOD". PSALMS 9:17. GOD HAS THE BEST PLAN FOR ALL HUMANITY. GOD'S PLAN IS RECOGNIZED BY THE FOUNDERS.

ABORTION vs DISCIPLINE
JESUS DISCIPLINES THE MIND OF THE TEENAGER

Satan's plan or program in to day's culture is to take the lead in programming young minds to think radical thinking rather than the wisdom of God. It's "choice." If you stay in God's program you will win. Whatever comes your way, you will overcome all obstacles with the Word of God. This is largely the "ANTICHRIST GENERATION. In general this generation must be against principles, morals and values of yesterday. The end result is you have corruption and destruction galore. MOST OF THE PROBLEMS ARE "MIND" RELATED ONLY ONE THING CAN FIX THESE BROKEN VESSELS , IT'S THE WORD OF GOD. IT CAN NOT BE FIXED BY HUMAN INTERVENTION ALONE WE HAVE TO HAVE A NEW BIRTH. YOU MUST BE BORN AGAIN BEFORE YOU SELF DESTRUCT OR IMPLODE. ALL THESE BEHAVIORS THE BIBLE CALLS SIN WILL BE BURNED WITH FIRE BUT THOSE IN CHRIST WILL SUFFER NO LOSS. WE HAVE A WHOLE PARTY GIVEN OVER TO CORRUPTION AND BEHAVIOR THAT IS TOTALLY UNAMERICAN. EVEN THE GOVERNMENT IS CORRUPT WITH A PRESIDENT THAT'S AGAINST THE SUPREME COURT, BIG ON KILLING BABIES, AND ABSENT FROM CLOSING OUR BORDERS

IT DOES MATTER WHAT YOU LEARN TO BELIEVE

We live in a world of GOOD and EVIL With the proper training children can become model citizens. That is , children grow up with sound mind and body. We've had over 200 years of practice with aminimum deviation from what we have always recognized as normal. The irony is that those who should be teaching boys how to be men, are themselves wearing dresses. No, they haven't become women, they just lost their mind. It's by design that the "left" want to strip away everything that's good, everything that's straight they want to bend it or break it because they have the mind of satan. They are poisoned by the music, drugs, failure to thrive, failure to learn positive concepts, failure to plan, failure to set goals especially regarding family, child bearing motherhood and fatherhood. If you have relation with the opposite sex, the likelihood of pregnancy is very real. FATHERS ARE GIVEN HEAVY RESPONSIBILIT BY BIBLICAL MANDATGE CONCERNING

HIS SEED. MEN ARE NOT EXCUSED FROM THE ABORTION DECISION SHE DID NOT MAKE THE BABY BY HERSELF YES, IT' S A BABY. NOT A BLOB, OR JUST A BATCH OF TISSUE. IT'S NOT A CAT OR A DOG, IT'S A BABY. THE NEXT LIE, IS THAT ABORTION IS REPRODUCTIVE HEALT???? NO, ABORTION IS NOTHING ABOUT HEALTH, ABORTION IS ABOUT KILLING. The relationship students develop with JESUS early in life will protect them throughout life's experience. It does matter what you think. An ounce of wrong thinking can cost you gallons of tears in sorrow. PARENTS, it is critical from day one that you build a proper foundation for learning, behavior and discipline. It is the best time to learn biblical principles and how God expects us to live. Repetition is the key to learning so tell them over and over again God loves us. Follow the Deuteronomy chapter 6 model for teaching.

<u>WHAT'S UP WITH ABORTION ANYWAY?? ISN'T THERE OTHE CHOICES??</u>

<u>GOD HAS PROVIDED THE SURE WAY TO REPRODUCTIVE HEALTH AND LIFE.</u> Abstinence is the best choice and it is attainable through a firm decision between both parties. Satan and the culture and sex mad individuals mark this decision as unrealistic, impossible and beyond control. This book is dedicated to believers who believe they can do all things through CHRIST who gives power to make the impossible possible. Everyone does not have the gift to abstain.

However, that doesn't mean you don't have control. You too can do all things through CHRIST. Remember, you can do what you set your mind to do by FAITH. THERE ARE GREAT REWARDS FOR OVERCOMING THE FLESH AND THE DEVIL. STRENGTH AND GREATNESS IS PROVEN BY BATTLES YOU WIN AND OBSTACLES YOU OVERCOME.

1. **CELIBATE – ABSTAINING FROM MARRIAGE AND SEXUAL RELATIONS, TYPICALLY FOR RELIGIOUS REASONS a celibate priest**

2. **Abstinent – usually refers to the decision not to have penetrative sex. It's typically limited to a specific period of time such as until marriage.**

THERE IS YET AN ALTERNATIVE TO ABORTION LET'S FACE IT. ABORTION HAS NOTHING TO DO WITH HEALTH: THE BABY DIES. HOW CAN THAT BE HEALTH?? ABORTION IS THE DOCTRINE OF SATAN. ITS' PURPOSE WAS

TO CONTROL THE POPULATION OF BLACK CHILDREN AND GENERATE BILLIONS IN CASH.

WHAT IF OUR YOUNG PEOPLE WERE GIVEN SPECIAL EDUCATION IN THE PROCESS OF REPRODUCTION? INSTEAD OF ABORTION, CONTROL. PUT THEM INCHARGE OF THEIR BODIES SO THEY WILL KNOW "WHEN" TO DO "WHAT". I CALL ON THE CHURCH TO EXPLORE THIS AREA AND AGREE ON WHAT PROCEDURES CAN BE PUT IN PLACE TO EDUCATE OUR YOUNG WOMEN AND TRAIN YOUNG MEN TO RESPECT THEIR SISTERS' POSITIVE CHOICE. WITH A LITTLE CARE AND SELF PRESERVATION YOU MAY HAVE THROUGH PREVENTION WHAT YOU CAN NEVER ACCOMPLISH THROUGH ABORTION.

LEARN BABY LEARN

<u>YOU CAN LEARN HOW TO CONTROL THE OUTCOME OF YOUR TRYST.</u>
Believers who are grounded in the Word of God have already talked over the direction of their relationship. They have set goals and drawn lines that they have agreed not to cross. Fulfillment of these commitments pay high dividends. One that cannot delay gratification for a glorious future does not meet the quality test. If you find that you are vulnerable and overly sensitive to touch, rather than subject yourself to an unwanted pregnancy, you should take steps well in advance of an encounter to control the outcome without abortion or abortion pills. Both parties should get a good lesson in biology as it relates to the reproductive process. DON'T CALL ABORTION REPRODUCTIVE HEALTH. "IT'S MURDER" IN THE FINAL ANALYSIS, THE BABY DIES. GET WITH YOUR PARENTS, YOUR TEACHER, YOUR DOCTOR OR REGISTERED NURSE, MAYBE THE SCHOOL DISTRICT WILL OFFER CLASSES IN AVOIDING PREGNANCY FROM A BIOLOGICAL STANDPOINT. IN THE END IT'S A PERSONAL RESPONSIBILITY.

THE IDEA HERE IS TO STOP KILLING BABIES. THE CHURCH EXPECTS BELIEVERS TO LISTEN AND REASON TOGETHER. If you are with someone that's wild, unreasonable and impatient, get out of that relation quickly. You do well to learn all you can about your body functions and how to have those functions working in your best interest, for your future and for your place in life. STOP AND THINK. HAVING PEADCE WITH A CLEAR CONSCIOUS IS PRICELESS. BE AN EXPERT AT TIME MANAGEMENT. DON'T BE PRESSURED INTO SOMETHING YOU ARE NOT READY FOR. THINK,

DREAM, INVISION, HOW DO YOU SEE YOURSELF NOW, TOMORROW, AND THROUGHOUT LIFEL. DELAY GRATIFICATION UNTIL THE TIME IS RIGHT. PLAN YOUR LIFE AND LIVE YOUR PLAN. THE WOMAN HAS GREAT INFLUENCE IN CONTROLING MORALITY. ONE JEWISH

PHILOSOPHER SAID: "A NATION IS NO GREATER THAN THE MORALS OF ITS' WOMEN. A PROFOUND "NO" MEANS "NO".THIS SOCIETY IS GREATLY INFLUENCED BY DEMONIC FORCES POSSESSING OR CONFUSING THE MIND OF THOSE THAT ARE WEAK. SEX CHANGE OPERATIONS ARE OF THE DEVIL. THOSE WHO CONDONE IT AND THE GOVERNMENT THAT DEFENDS IT ARE CORRUPT AND CONFUSED. SAVE YOURSELF FROM THIS WICKED GENERATION. THE PROBLEM IS NOT RACIAL IT'S GOOD AGAINST EVIL. IT'S THE ANTI-CHRIST SPIRIT. THEY FIGHT AGAINST THE VALUES THAT JESUS TAUGHT.

TAKE A LOOK AT THE BIOLOGY AND LEARN THE ABC's

The average menstrual cycle lasts 28 days. The cycle starts with the first day of one period and ends with the first day of the next period. The average woman ovulates on day 14. **GET HELP FROM A QUALIFIED PERSON: MOTHER, TEACHER, NURSE, DOCTOR.**

KNOW THE DAYS TO GET PREGNANT – FIGURE OUT WHEN YOU OVULATE . AVOID UNWANTED PROGNANCY. AVOID ABORTION. HAVE A CLEAR CONSCIOUS.